HELP YOUR
CHILD
TO READ
BETTER

HELP YOUR CHILD TO READ BETTER

JAMES
SCHIAVONE

Nelson-Hall nh Chicago

Books by James Schiavone
You Can Read Faster
Seven Keys to a Richer Vocabulary
How to Pass Exams

Library of Congress Cataloging in Publication Data

Schiavone, James.
Help your child to read better.

Bibliography: p.
Includes index.
1. Reading—Remedial teaching. I. Title.
LB1050.5.S29   372.4'3   76–29055
ISBN 0-88229-221-8 (cloth)
ISBN 0-88229-464-4 (paper)

Manufactured in the United States of America.

For
Isabel, Francine, Cheryl, Christine,
Patrice, Michael, and Jennifer

CONTENTS

Acknowledgments   ix
Introduction   xi

PART I   The Reading Process
Chapter 1
The Reading Problem   3
Your Attitudes as a Parent ● What is Dyslexia?
● Functional Behavior Problems ● How You Can Help
Your Child at Home ● Questions and Answers
Chapter 2
What is Reading?   15
Chapter 3
Getting Ready to Read   18
Learning to Look ● What Parents Can Do ● Learning
to Walk—Physical Skills and Maturity ● Learning to
Talk ● Hearing ● The Skill of Listening ●
● Questions and Answers
Chapter 4
How Your Child Learns to Read   30
Questions and Answers

PART II   Reading in the Elementary School
Chapter 5
Reading in the Primary Grades   37

How are Children Taught to Read? ● Reading Readiness
● Judging Reading Readiness ● Visit Your School ●
How to Help Your Child Achieve Reading Readiness
● Prereading Games ● Phonics Versus the Look-Say
Method ● Skills in Word Recognition ● Difficulties and
Problems in the Teaching of Phonics ● How are Phonics
Taught in the Schools? ● Other Primary Reading Skills
● Approaches to the Teaching of Reading ● *The Basal
Reader Approach* ● *The Language Experience
Approach* ● *The Linguistics Approach* ● *The
Phonetic-Alphabet Approach* ● *The Programmed
Learning Approach* ● Games to Help Your Child in
Phonics ● More Word Games ● Questions and Answers

Chapter 6
Reading in the Intermediate Grades   70
Reading Interests ● Games to Play ● Questions
and Answers

PART III   **Reading in the Secondary School**
Chapter 7
The Adolescent Years   83
Vocabulary Development ● Comprehension Skills ●
Skills Used in Studying ● Reading in Mathematics,
Science, and the Social Sciences ● Reading Rate
● Developmental Reading ● Corrective Reading ●
Remedial Reading

Chapter 8
Teenage Reading Problems
and What to Do About Them   99
Factors in the Home ● Problems in Reading ● The
Reluctant Reader ● Poor Comprehension ●
Questions and Answers

Books for Parents   107
Books for Children   109
Books for Teenagers   114
Index   117

Grateful acknowledgment is made to the many parents whose questions and concerns have formed the basis for the development of this book. I am especially indebted to Milvy Bryant who typed the manuscript and assisted in preparing it for publication.

INTRODUCTION

Is it your responsibility as a parent to teach your child to read? Obviously the major responsibility for all academic instruction belongs to the schools. They are specifically set up for instructional purposes and have the facilities, materials, and the skills and abilities of highly trained personnel to guide your child in the development of his academic learning processes. The schools also reinforce your child's emotional and social development. It is not, then, your responsibility as a parent to sit down night after night with instructional materials and attempt to teach your child the things he should be learning at school.

However, the responsibility of the school, as great as it may be, is indeed limited when weighed against your responsibility as a parent. As a parent you are undoubtedly interested in the total development of your child. The fact that you are reading this book provides sufficient evidence of that commitment. The total development of your child includes factors relating to his health and nutrition and his general well-being, in addition to his education. Obviously his education does not begin and end at the school door. What you do to provide a home environment conducive to learning and study enables you to meet, in part, your responsibilities for your child's education. These pages contain information that will assist you in fulfilling that responsibility.

You have probably heard or read that instruction in reading has actually improved during the last forty years. If this is the case, you may be wondering, why have we so many poor readers today? The National Education Association has statistics which indicate that there are fewer poor readers today than there were forty years ago. This is based on comparisons of numbers of students attending school then and now. Years ago poor readers simply dropped out of school. Today there are more students in school, and they are staying in school even if they have problems in reading. The NEA statistics are supported by standardized tests in reading. Tests given only recently show equal or somewhat higher comprehension in reading for today's children as compared with results of the same tests administered more than thirty years ago. This is in spite of the fact that there are many children in school today who because of reading problems would have dropped out of school back in the twenties and thirties.

Students who are in school only because of our compulsory education laws constitute the major portion of the problem readers. There was a time when students merely failed in history or geography. These were the drop-outs. Today students are more likely to have problems in reading, and to remain in school. Actually, many of today's boys and girls are learning to read well, to read widely, and to enjoy many books. Of course there will always be room for improvement of instruction in reading. Such improvement will occur as more and more information is uncovered regarding the psychology of reading. Chapter 2 presents in-depth information on the process of reading.

This book is intended for you, the parent, whether your child is reading below his grade level, at grade level, or is showing above average skill in reading. Since reading is such a highly complex process, your child may be average or better than average in some skills and deficient in others. Or perhaps your child is deficient in all of the reading skills and is therefore unable to make satisfactory progress at school. Whatever your child's present reading skills and abilities happen to be, this book will help you to develop a "home-program" tailored to his specific needs.

This home-program is not one with long wearisome drills designed to bore your child, create a dislike for reading, and frazzle your own nerves to the point of frustration and hopelessness. Neither is it a cure-all method. Some critics of our schools have strongly urged that a phonetic approach be employed exclusively to solve all problems in reading. The process of reading is too complex to be reduced to one method guaranteed to make all children superior readers. As far back as 1838, Horace Mann, the Secretary of the Board of Education for Massachusetts, stated in a report, "More than eleven-twelfths of all the children in the reading classes in our schools do not understand the meaning of the words they read." Interestingly enough this observation was made at a time when phonics instruction was the reading method most often used. A discussion of phonics versus the look-say method is presented in Chapter 5.

The first step in the success of any home-program has to do with your attitudes and habits as a parent. Your understanding of your child and his problems will greatly influence the manner in which he grows and matures. A positive, understanding attitude toward your child makes for better learning conditions. Have you noticed how some children blossom out under the guidance of a wise and sympathetic teacher? Such a teacher takes an active interest in his students and provides tasks that have meaning and significance for them. He enables his students to experience success, believing in the old adage "Nothing succeeds like success." Such a teacher knows that learning cannot take place without the proper psychological conditions. He loves children and is sympathetic and understanding toward them. He sets the conditions for learning.

Parents of preschool and first-grade children often ask the question "At what age do children learn to read?" The answer is that a child will learn to read when he is ready. A specific chronological age cannot be designated that is applicable to all children. Reading is a developmental task comparable to the infant's development of vision and his mastery of crawling, walking, and talking. Developmental tasks are described further in Chapter 3. Some children learn to read faster than others. While some will begin reading in the first grade, others will not learn to read until second or third grade.

Variations among children learning to read are produced by several major factors: mental, social and emotional, physical, and educational. These factors are interrelated and must all be considered in assessing a child's readiness to read. A weakness in one area may be compensated by a strength in another. However, some problems may lead to other weaknesses. A hearing problem may retard speech and vocabulary development, which in turn affects reading readiness. The modern technology of teaching reading places importance on when to begin instruction. Readiness may be considered as the first step in learning to read.

This book explains readiness and offers concrete suggestions as to what you can do about helping your child get ready to read. Another purpose of this book is to provide you with a background of information necessary to aid you in determining your role in the development of your child's reading skills. It provides many suggestions from which you may select those appropriate to your child. The questions and answers will present you with a quick and easy point of reference. Our overall purpose is to enable you to develop a sound and confident background in working with teachers to help your child to read better.

PART I

The Reading Process

Chapter 1

The Reading Problem

Why should reading ever constitute a problem for any child? Perhaps the answer to this question lies in the fact that reading is the most complex task facing children in early life. Fortunately most children are able to accomplish this task as a part of their natural growth in learning. But while some children will learn just enough to get by, others will become superior readers and will continue to develop this skill in their adult years.

The importance of reading cannot be overemphasized. It is the foundation of all major learning activities in school and in future life. One can learn some things through listening and actual performance, but how far can one get without reading? It is no wonder, then, that parents often show a strong interest in their children's reading. Many parents have become concerned over the various methods they hear and read about concerning the teaching of reading. Conflicting points of view in newspapers, magazines, and books add to the general confusion.

Every generation produces its poor readers. Because of the recent trends in science and technology, and compulsory education through the age of sixteen, problems in reading have been brought to the attention of all of us. Such attention is all to the good. An awareness of problems and difficulties in education leads to research in an effort to uncover the solutions to these problems.

America provides innumerable cultural advantages for its citizens, and such advantages are reflected in modern-day education. Learning has always taken place long before the child enters school. Today the learning process is further enhanced through radio, television, films, records, and other nonprint media.

Amidst all of this, whom are we to blame for the problems in reading? Our first reaction is to pinpoint the school as the primary source of these problems. Yet an analysis of the situation discloses that there are important factors other than the school which contribute to problems in reading. The home, for instance, constitutes the central point of the child's life and the conditions there greatly affect his learning processes.

Your Attitudes as a Parent

Your attitudes as a parent have a direct influence on your child's progress in reading. Sam Levinson tells a story about his mother's reaction to a 98 percent which he brought home on his report card. She looked at the grade and then looked back at Sam, asking, "And who got the other 2 percent?" Levinson goes on to tell us that when his mother's presence was requested at school she would lead him by the ear to the teacher. She would then slap his face and turn to the teacher, asking, "Now just what is it you wanted to see me about?"

These stories have parental attitudes as their basis. It sometimes appears to a child that despite his achievements his parents do not adequately demonstrate their satisfaction. Children need and enjoy recognition when they accomplish certain tasks well.

There are several parental attitudes which can be detrimental to a child's growth. Pride and indifference are two of them. Parents who engage in too much boasting about their child's achievements may cause unnecessary embarrassment to a sensitive child. It is possible for such a child to feel that his parents view his scholastic achievements as being more important than he is. Such feelings can result in a lack of effort and cause the child to become an underachiever.

Indifference, on the other hand, can have an equally adverse effect. The child may feel he is not getting the attention he deserves and may therefore fail to work up to his potential.

Anxiety accompanied by overindulgence can be very destructive to a child's development. Anxiety may cause parents to put pressure on a child. This pressure may manifest itself in the parents trying to tutor the child, taking away his privileges, having him tested and retested, taking him from one specialist to another, and promising him gifts contingent upon a satisfactory report from school.

Natural anxiety of course can serve as an encouragement to succeed. But strong anxiety is an unfavorable and disturbing attitude which distracts the child from the learning process.

Among the parental attitudes which favor the child's development are a genuine respect for the child as a person, an understanding of his progress in reading and learning, and an expectation that he will do his best. By focusing on the child's positive attributes, giving him the credit and praise he deserves, and treating him in a firm, consistent, and just manner, a parent can help a child to achieve his potential.

What Is Dyslexia?

In modern education we must raise the question, "Can all children learn to read?" Most children will learn to do some reading with proper instruction. Because of individual differences some children will learn very little and there are situations and conditions in which some children will never learn to read. A serious reading disability called dyslexia is loosely defined as the inability of an apparently normal child of adequate intelligence and with no marked or special visual problems to learn how to read, even with adequate instruction. It is in effect a label, and a very formidable one, that terrorizes and threatens parents.

A pure case of dyslexia, as defined here, would be hard

to find. It is in fact rare to run into the case of a child whose reading disability can not be explained in terms of some understandable basis. Actually specialists have not clearly defined dyslexia or described its causation. In a paper entitled "Dyslexia: A Discussion of its Definition," prepared for the Second Meeting of the Federal Government's Attack on Dyslexia (Washington, D.C.: Bureau of Research, U.S. Office of Education, August, 1967), Richard Adams concluded, "sometimes a word gets born which, rather than live as a servant to man, moves out in life like a Frankenstein monster wreaking havoc in the discourse of sensible men. *Dyslexia* is such a word. Its sound is noxious, its meaning is obscure, it has divided the efforts of honest men when collaboration would have been the better course."

The term *dyslexia* therefore does not appear to be a useful one. It is not useful to label a child as *dyslexic,* or anything else for that matter, unless the label is used as a preliminary step toward some kind of positive action. Among those using the term *dyslexia* there is no unanimity of agreement regarding definition. Some hold that the term is broadly equivalent to "reading disability." Others hold that it is a congenital or inherited condition with certain identifiable characteristics. Still others attribute its etiology to brain damage. A reading disability may well be the result of psychoneurological conditions in which the central nervous system does not function effectively in sensory-motor, perceptual-motor, or language functions. Such malfunctioning may be due to genetic and/or maturational conditions, traumatic experiences, emotional problems, or any combination of these.

Researchers have conducted intensive studies of the causal factors in severe reading disability. Naturally not all causal factors identified appear in every case of reading disability; each factor present is more or less intense depending upon the particular case diagnosed. Such studies indicate certain possible causal factors as visual difficulties, neurological problems, speech and auditory difficulties, social and emotional problems, endocrine disturbances, general physical difficulties, and poor teaching methods.

Studies in the etiology of reading disability presently lead to the conclusion that there are some cases in which neurological immaturity or damage is a definite factor, but that there are many additional factors that can handicap a child in learning to read. Therefore, any child who does not respond to remedial teaching techniques (and may possibly be labeled *dyslexic*), should be thoroughly diagnosed by competent specialists to uncover those significant handicaps contributing to the reading disability. There are special teaching techniques that may be employed.

Most parents who suspect that their child is dyslexic want to find out as much as they can about this condition and often ask educators to pinpoint the problem. Why is it that an otherwise normal child may experience difficulty in comprehending words and symbols? This basic question may remain unsolved until we have a better understanding from a neurological standpoint of how the mind works and how children learn to read and write. How is it that a child, or even an adult for that matter, can look at a word and see some of the letters reversed, inverted, or transposed? This behavior caused defective vision to become a prime suspect in the early attempts to explain dyslexia. We cannot dismiss this as a possible causal factor, but poor eyesight alone cannot be the primary cause of dyslexia. In studying eye movements in reading, opthalmologists have concluded that faulty eye movements (left-to-right direction) are the result, not the cause, of inability to recognize printed symbols and words. Although this inability is a visual perception problem, the difficulties arise from the manner in which the brain interprets the visual stimuli from the eyes. What goes wrong in the brain remains the unanswered question. Brain damage could result in dyslexia, but does not appear to be a common cause of the condition. Brain injuries that would involve only those areas concerned with language factors would be relatively rare. Why is it that more left-handed and ambidextrous children demonstrate symptoms of dyslexia? Why is it that more boys are dyslexic? There are subtle factors other than brain damage per se that may underlie the condition. A difficult birth, protein deficiencies, oxygen deprivation, and air and food pollution may all be suspect but none can be pinpointed as a primary cause. Whatever the contributing causes are, we must return to the vexing question of why the damage focuses on only the language and symbol manipulation areas of the brain, without harming the reasoning power areas.

A widely held theory on the cause of dyslexia is that related to delayed maturation or the so-called late bloomer. The late bloomer is a child whose reading readiness stage does not develop as early as others'. This lack of early development may be due to a condition of mixed or confused brain dominance. Normally one side of the brain becomes dominant in the use of language. When this does not occur we have instead a condition of faulty patterning of brain function wherein both hemispheres of the brain compete with each other. This causes reversed, transposed, or inverted perception in relation to the printed page. A confused or mixed brain dominance could cause the symptoms of dyslexia. As a parent you should be aware of the trouble signs of this language learning disability. Following is a list of eight trouble signs as reported by the National Reading Center, Washington, D.C.

1. Dyslexic children are more often boys than girls.
2. They evidence intact senses, a culturally adequate home, normal intelligence, and freedom from gross neurological defect.
3. They usually come from families where there is a history of learning difficulties.
4. They are unable to learn even after extensive exposure to conventional teaching techniques.
5. They have great difficulty in remembering whole words and do not learn easily by the sight method of instruction.
6. Their spelling is poor and their handwriting is slow, cramped, and barely legible.
7. They demonstrate reversals and rotations of let-

ters and words. These reversals are common and very often persist throughout the grades.

8. They may be good in arithmetic in the early grades, but eventually they are poor in all subjects that require reading.

Practice has demonstrated that certain remedial techniques do work in helping a dyslexic child. Such a child can learn to read at a reasonable rate with excellent comprehension. There are many approaches to remediate dyslexia. Some techniques involve physical development programs consisting of eye exercises, walking along a balance beam, bouncing on a trampoline, creeping and crawling exercises, and the use of machines to develop visual perception. Other techniques may employ a phonetic alphabet, a color-coded alphabet, writing in sand, tracing letters and words with the finger, and principles of phonics. All of these techniques bring into play the child's senses of seeing, hearing, and touching. The child may look at a word, hear its pronunciation, trace it in a sand tray, in the air, or on the blackboard, feel a three-dimensional cutout of the letters, and so forth.

What is needed for the dyslexic child is individualized tutoring. The key to success in dealing with the problem lies in a careful fitting of techniques and materials to the particular child's needs. Unfortunately, there is no one method of teaching reading to all dyslexic readers. The right methods are those that work for the particular child.

Two widely used teaching techniques involving a multisensory approach are known as the Fernald method and the Gillingham method. The Fernald technique allows the child to watch and listen while a word is written. He then traces the word while pronouncing it. As he makes progress he can write the word directly without tracing, pronouncing it as he writes it. Through this approach he begins to learn whole words. This kinesthetic technique has been successful with many seriously dyslexic readers. The Gillingham method employs letter sounds which are subsequently built into words. The method enables the child to make associations between the sounds of the letters and the way they appear, and eventually how they are blended together.

Functional Behavior Problems

A child with reading difficulties often exhibits severe behavior problems at home and at school. The child with Functional Behavior Problems (FBP) is almost constantly engaged in purposeless activity. He is aggressive, destructive, and is easily frustrated. His attention span is very brief and he has difficulty in concentrating on specific tasks. The FBP child is intelligent, but he performs poorly in school. Although he wants very much to make friends, his behavior and attitudes are such that his peers shun him. His teachers and parents as well as his playmates find his behavior difficult to cope with.

The FBP child is not an isolated occurrence. Experts estimate that as many as two million children may be affected by this syndrome. This is little consolation for parents of such children, but it is important to note that FBP exists and it does affect the child's learning and social development. In FBP there are no detectable pathological conditions that would account for the behavior; doctors have ruled out epilepsy, brain tumor, neurosis, schizophrenia, and retardation as causative factors. The etiology of FBP is not fully understood. Like dyslexia, it uses various terms to identify the condition. Some of these, such as "hyperkinetic syndrome," "hyperactive child syndrome," and "minimal brain dysfunction," are also used to describe causative factors of dyslexia.

The FBP syndrome is characterized by a number of signs:

• Overactivity—the child is full of energy, can't stop talking, constantly disturbs his teacher and playmates, disrupts the classroom, and can't seem to keep his hands to himself.

• Low frustration tolerance—the child is easily frustrated, pays no attention in school, is impatient when he has to look or listen, and moves erratically from one activity to another.

• Aggressiveness—the child is apt to take risks without thought of consequence. He is destructive, starts fights with his peers, and bullies smaller children. This aggressiveness frequently gets him into trouble with his teacher and peers.

• Irritability—the child is highly irritable and unpredictable, throws temper tantrums, and is rebellious, hostile, and stubborn.

• Underachiever—the child does not work up to his potential at school, even though he is of average or above average intelligence.

The key to helping the FBP child is to recognize the problem. Early diagnosis and treatment is extremely important. Your doctor is the best person to advise you if your child is hyperkinetic. He may after thorough diagnosis prescribe medication to control hyperactivity. You should follow your doctor's advice and his directions. School authorities should be informed if the child is undergoing therapy for hyperactivity. They will certainly want to cooperate with you and your physician.

How You Can Help Your Child at Home

As stated earlier, the material in this book has not been prepared to enable you to take over the teacher's job. Instead you will find many specific suggestions about reinforcing the school's program of instruction in order to help your child at home. Following are some basic preliminary generalizations for your consideration. In later chapters you will be given additional information to implement your efforts.

• As a part of your child's early preschool development you can help him develop his language usage, vocabulary, and cognition.

• You can help your child by safeguarding his physical and mental health and development through periodic examinations by the family physician. You should be aware of vision and hearing difficulties, if any, prior to entering your child in first grade.

• You should provide an abundance of books and reading materials for your child.

• By working with your child's interests and hobbies, you can help to stimulate further interest by having him read about these activities.

• You can see to it that your child is exposed to the games and activities that will aid him in his reading experiences. Such games and activities are suggested in this book.

• You can keep in touch with your child's teacher so that you will be aware of the kinds of progress taking place.

• You can maintain a home atmosphere conducive to learning.

These are just a few of the general ways in which you can help your child to better reading. Details will be discussed in later chapters.

Questions and Answers

Should a child of five show a strong degree of enthusiasm for learning to read? An enthusiasm for learning to read at age five is indeed desirable. This enthusiasm comes as a result of the child's normal development. However, we cannot pinpoint a particular age at which this desire should manifest itself. Each child is an individual and children will not all achieve the same things at the same time in their development. In any event their early experiences at home will eventually lead to a desire to learn to read.

A very rapid period of language development and growth occurs in the child from three to six. He begins to ask many questions and enjoys using and playing with words. His interests begin to develop and to focus on himself and his world. He begins to distinguish between what is real and what is imaginary.

This development in your child offers you an avenue of approach toward stimulating his interests and his enthusiasm for reading. You may even be unaware of some of the things that you do that may cause your child to learn to love reading and to want to read. The child has seen you reading and he concludes that you derive pleasure from doing this. As you read to him the stories which he loves, he learns that those black symbols on the page have meaning. The nursery rhymes and poems with their rhyming words and repetitions delight him and kindle his enthusiasm for books and reading. He enjoys the fuzzy feel and the bright colors of the pictures. In selecting books for your child keep in mind his play and social interests. The more you expose your child to reading-related activities, the greater his enthusiasm will be for reading.

How can I determine if my child is a retarded reader? A retarded reader is anyone who is not reading as well as his capabilities permit. If your child has the ability to read better than he does, there are a number of indications to help you determine this fact. If he is doing well in subjects that do not require much reading, and if he experiences success at school despite a low reading level, these are indications of a higher reading potential. If he appears to act his age, get along with members of his peer group, and is able to remember and relate stories he has heard, he probably has a reading potential higher than his actual achievement.

Your child's teacher should be able to help him to overcome his deficiencies. If not, the teacher may request the services of a specialist. The two of them might have some specific suggestions for you in helping your child at home.

If I discover that my child is seriously behind in his reading, what can I do to help? In such a situation your best bet is to leave the job of instruction to the teacher or specialist. Any attempt you might make at instruction will probably only serve to strain relations between your child and his teacher.

You will have to show your child that you understand his problem and that you appreciate his efforts to do the best he can. A relaxed home atmosphere in which you and your child are engaged in activities other than reading instruction will do much to facilitate the job of the teacher. Of course if your child or teenager asks for specific help, this should be offered.

Should I make my child read? If I do not force him to read won't he continue to fall behind? As a parent you certainly cannot allow your child to do anything he pleases when he pleases. On the other hand, being a strict disciplinarian may lead to other problems. You should of course maintain control and set certain limitations. You will have to exercise your own judgment as to how much time your child should spend with his books. Obviously neglect of the development of reading skills will not help the child to move ahead. He could possibly fall behind if little or no emphasis is placed on reading and school work. Encouraging a child to reach some of his more immediate goals can provide the needed push.

Chapter 2

What is Reading?

Volumes have been written on the topic of reading. That is because of the many complex actions which take place in this process. The purpose of this brief chapter is to give you, the parent, some valuable background information and insight into the dynamic activity of reading. This will lead you to a clearer understanding of the task of the school and set the stage for the chapters to follow. Although this chapter is somewhat technical, an effort has been made to present the subject in general terms.

The process of reading combines both psychological and physiological functions. When a person is confronted with the printed page, both of these functions are brought into play. Perhaps the easiest way to look at the total process is to consider the essential factors involved and to depict them as they occur sequentially and as they relate and interact with each other. What takes place when we read must of necessity be a repetitious and cyclical process. It is a continuous cycle of visual stimuli and mental reactions, conveying sequences of ideas into meaningful, intelligible patterns.

For purposes of simplification and clarity we can break down the process of reading into four sequential steps:

(1) Seeing—This is the physiological process of looking at the printed page. The light reflected from around the print is picked up by the light-sensitive nerves in the eyes and is transmitted to the brain.

(2) Perceiving—This is the psychological process during which the reader becomes aware of the words and their sequence on the printed page. The reader associates the words with their meanings and is aware of the patterns of language which the words convey.

(3) Understanding—In this step there is an overlapping of processes. In fact all of the steps are interrelated and overlapping. Understanding is of course related to perceiving, and is a continuation of the process in which word sequences are translated into meaning. This meaning or understanding is arrived at through one or several of the thought processes—categorizing, comparing, forming visual and other sensory impressions, and reacting to what is read.

In the process of understanding the reader brings all of his experience and background to the printed page. Since reading is an active process the reader reacts to what is read. He does not merely absorb what is written.

(4) Interpretation, Evaluation, Application, Appreciation—In this step the reader has already comprehended the meaning and has otherwise reacted to the material. Now the reader interprets what he has read by relating the content to his own background and experience. Through critical analysis he evaluates the material by considering the author's background, his tone, the factual content of his work, and so forth.

There are more than thirty separate processes of seeing, perceiving, understanding and reacting involved in the total process of reading. These complex processes are repetitive and overlapping so that they are not easily separated, but they have been recognized. Years of research into the psychology of reading has enabled educators to examine this highly complex process and to understand its nature. This understanding has led to many of the modern techniques employed in the teaching of reading. It is important for parents to know about the various steps in the reading process in order to understand the methods employed in the school.

Chapter 3

Getting Ready to Read

Reading is a developmental task, one which the individual must learn in steps. Robert Havighurst, in his book *Developmental Tasks and Education,* gives the following definition:

> A developmental task is a task which arises at or about a certain period in the life of the individual, successful achievement of which leads to his happiness and to success with later tasks, while failure leads to unhappiness in the individual, disapproval by the society, and difficulty with later tasks.

A brief look at some of the developmental tasks of infancy and early childhood will aid in understanding the process of learning to read in middle childhood.

Learning to Look

There are some basic facts which you should know about your child's vision. This information should help you to make practical decisions where your child's vision is concerned. Visual development begins at birth and continues up to adulthood. This development constitutes an important factor in the success or failure of the child in school and at play. A prerequisite to word recognition and success in reading is adequate vision.

The eye is a complicated organ with many constituents working together to produce vision. If all parts do not work in conjunction with each other the quality of the retinal impression is affected. A definition of terms will be helpful to this discussion. *Acuity* is the ability to see clearly and distinctly. *Accommodation* is the ability of the eye to focus or to adjust in order to bring an image into sharp focus. *Fusion* represents a state of single vision in which the images from the two eyes are merged with sufficient quality to be realized as one image only. *Binocular coordination* is the capability of using the two eyes as a team in a manner of movement that is sufficiently coordinated to permit and maintain fusion, as during the process of reading. *Motility* refers to the ease or facility with which a reader makes ocular rotations, those left to right movements the eyes make while reading along a line of print.

Common problems of visual acuity are nearsightedness (myopia), farsightedness (hyperopia), and astigmatism. In myopia, conditions in the overall shape of the eye, the cornea, and the lens cause the rays of light entering the eye to come to a point in front of the retina resulting in a blurred image. Only when the rays of light are focused directly on the retina is the clearest acuity achieved, as occurs in the normal eye (see Figure 1). Myopia results in the inability to see clearly at a distance. The myopic child will often complain that he cannot see a sign or that he cannot see what his teacher writes on the chalkboard. If the condition occurs early in life, the child may not realize that he has a problem since what he sees appears to him to be normal. The condition can of course be corrected by glasses or contact lenses which permit the rays of light to fall properly on the retina.

Hyperopia on the other hand results in the inability to see clearly at a short distance, as in reading. In hyperopia, rays of light entering the eye come to a focus beyond the retina (see Figure 2). Note from the figure that the eye is too short. Because of this visual condition, the child may avoid pastimes requiring

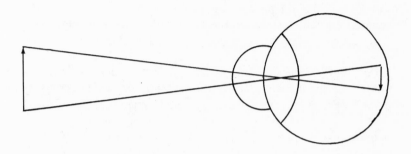

Figure 1.   Normal Eye

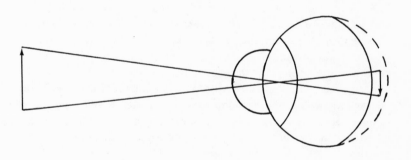

Figure 2.   Hyperopic Eye

close eye work and find interest in other activities such as sports. The tension on the muscles which control the lens during accommodation results in eyestrain in the hyperopic child. This often causes the child to just give up in his reading efforts. Since a hyperopic child can see well for short periods of time the condition may escape notice by parents and teachers. Hyperopia can also be corrected by glasses or contact lenses.

Astigmatism is caused by an uneven curvature of the cornea. This type of corneal curvature results in a blurred vision which causes the child to squint in order to see better. Astigmatism often accompanies conditions of myopia and hyperopia. It can often be corrected with proper glasses or contact lenses.

These common problems may affect each eye differently. Although each eye can be separately corrected, problems of *double vision* (diplopia) occur when the eyes do not work in unison to view a particular object or target area. It has been established that the visual conditions most important to the reading act are binocular coordination, visual fusion, and lateral and vertical eye muscle balance. In order to maintain single binocular vision and adequate fusion during reading, it is necessary for the reader to have sufficient *convergence,* the ability to rotate the eyes toward the nose in order to achieve the impingement of a given image on corresponding retinal areas. When double vision occurs due to improper binocular coordination the child may alternate viewing the target area, first with one eye and then the other. Or he may learn to suppress the vision in one eye and favor the other. This problem is generally missed in using the Snellen Chart, the familiar one with the large letters at the top and the smaller ones at the bottom, because the eyes are used separately in this test. Overconvergence of the eyes may result in a condition of *cross-eyedness*; underconvergence may result in a condition of *walleyedness.*

There are a variety of symptoms which your child may exhibit. These are clues to possible vision problems. If the child squints a lot, rubs his eyes frequently, or suffers from many sties, this may be an indication of a visual condition that should be corrected. If one eye persistently rotates in or out there may be a problem of binocular coordination. When your child reads, notice if he moves his head from left to right or if he tilts his head forward, backward, to one side, or shuts or covers one eye. All of these actions may be symptoms of visual problems, although they could be caused by other factors. All of the conditions described can be dealt with. Since the visual function is so necessary in school activities and since visual demands increase over the grades, periodic eye examinations are strongly recommended.

What Parents Can Do

At home you can help your child to develop visual skills before he starts school. For example, the baby has learned to distinguish many different objects before learning to talk. He knows the difference between ball, block, book, rattle, TV, shoes, and so forth, because he has been taught these things. In developing visual skills, the small child gets reinforcement through the other senses. He is developing readiness for reading as he begins to note the details of various objects, pictures, shapes, and colors. You can help your child by bringing to his attention foods, sounds, animals, toys, and people. The home provides the perfect learning laboratory for this kind of activity.

Here are some specific suggestions for assisting the learning and visual development of the child from two to six:

• Match various household items by size, shape, and color. Use cans, blocks, buttons, beads, spools, spoons, colored toothpicks, and macaroni in varied shapes.

• Collect pictures of animals, flowers, and toys. Compare and contrast them. Sort them into separate classification piles of food, furniture, flowers, clothing, and so forth.

• Identify various household objects by adjectives describing size, shape, texture, placement (the light is *over* the desk), and so forth.

By putting these suggestions into action, you have an excellent opportunity to help your child develop good visual discrimination and visual memory.

Learning to Walk—
Physical Skills and Maturity

Somewhere between nine and fifteen months of age the child is biologically ready to walk. Bones, muscles, and nerves have developed by this time to the point where the child can perform this task. When the basic skills of walking have been mastered, the child continues to grow and learns to jump, skip, and run. He learns to stretch, twist, turn, kick, pull, grab, throw, catch, and slide. His visual-motor coordination develops to a finer degree and he is able to perform more complex tasks. All kinds of physical activities and games help the child to control his body and to move about in his world.

No two children develop in quite the same manner. However, all children need space in which to play and exercise. Any opportunities that you can provide for your child that will strengthen his visual-motor coordination will allow him to develop his inherent capacities.

Providing the child with toys often aids in the development of his physical skills and maturity. In the crib the infant plays with his rattle and enjoys his crib mobile. Plastic and rubber squeezable toys enable him to reach, grab, squeeze, shake, and pull. At about one to two-and-one-half years of age the child enjoys the push-and-pull toys, form boards, plastic telephones, dolls, inflatable plastic riding toys, bouncing balls, and bean bags. These toys are still useful for children of two to four years of age, who also need to play on slides, swings, and in sandboxes. They may be provided with water toys, plastic dolls, dollhouses, toy cars and trucks, and tricycles.

From ages four to six, children continue to enjoy the aforementioned toys. During this time they like to engage in such physical activities as swimming, playing ball, hopscotch, and so forth. Some attention should be paid to small muscle control at this time. Such activities as stringing beads, lacing, buttoning, and tying are important to visual perception and concentration. Small muscle control is essential for learning to read and write. Some of the activities requiring small muscle control are often tiresome, so the child should be allowed to stop when he wants to. Let him play with pencils, crayons, chalk, coloring books, puzzles, modeling clay, silly-putty, finger paints, pegboards, scissors, and paste. When you bake, let your child measure, stir, pour, and mix. Supervise him in the use of hammer and nails, saw, and so forth. Use your creativity to come up with games, toys, and activities. All of these activities develop the important readiness for reading.

Learning to Talk

Biologically the child is ready to talk long before he actually begins to accomplish this task. His vocal apparatus is fairly well-developed at birth and is evidenced by the infant's healthy screaming and crying. The newborn child is able to make the sounds of the vowels short $\breve{e}$ and short $\breve{a}$, and also the consonants g and k.

As the people around him teach him to associate sounds with situations and objects, the child begins to shape words out of his infant babble. He gradually learns to associate the sounds of language with situations and experiences. As the child develops he learns the meanings of new sounds, although he may not use the words at this stage. From the age of eighteen months to about four years is the period of baby talk. During this time the child may leave out some consonant sounds. Throughout this period he is developing an oral vocabulary essential to his initial attempts at learning to read. This development will proceed normally provided there are no hearing defects. Be on the lookout for any hearing defects so they may be corrected or compensated for early.

From the age of three upward the child begins to expand his vocabulary and to learn proper grammatical structure. He also learns to associate past and present tense. Because he is confused by the illogical basis of grammatical structure, he says, "I drinked the milk," and "I catched the ball." He concludes that this is correct because from past experiences he noticed the addition of *ed* to indicate past action. However, in spite of the difficulties, he learns proper usage.

Hearing

Even a slight hearing loss may affect the child's ability to learn new vocabulary, gain ideas, and imitate correct speech sounds. He may have difficulty in distinguishing between initial and final consonants such as *b, v, t, d, ed,* and the vowel sounds in *mat* and *met.* Such auditory discrimination is necessary to successful instruction in phonics and spelling.

The most accurate measure of a child's auditory acuity is through an audiometer test. Gross difficulties in hearing may be detected through the whisper test or the watch test, but these techniques are not dependable. A child's hearing should be checked periodically. You should look for persistent signs of hearing difficulty such as lack of attention, needing to have words and phrases repeated, tilting the head to hear better, and playing the TV or radio at high volume.

The Skill of Listening

If your child is to be successful at school he must be able to listen attentively and to follow simple directions. Since so much of the instruction he will get at school is oral, his listening ability will be an important factor in learning to read. When you listen attentively as your child relates a radio or television program or tells about his play experiences with children in the neighborhood, you encourage good listening skills. At the same time your child should learn to understand that it is important to listen to you and to follow your directions and requests.

There are many fine recordings made especially for children. You can provide these records to help your child increase his ability to listen attentively. You will also open a new world of music and stories for him. Children's records abound and some of them are quite good. Records for preschoolers should not have harsh tones. They should be clear and pleasant to the ear. They should be of the interest level and comprehension level suitable to the child's age. You can provide your child with a wide variety of records. Select some stories for humor, suspense, and adventure. Get some animal stories, fairy tales, and musical stories. Children love to clap, sing, and dance, so get some march and dance tunes. Other records teach the alphabet, counting, basic concepts such as big-little, up-down, heavy-light, and so forth.

Following are some selections which are suggested as a starting point. *My First Golden Record Library* is by Golden Records and is distributed by Affiliated Publishers, New York. This set consists of twelve volumes and contains such recordings as Mother Goose rhymes, fairy tales, animal songs, nursery songs, folk songs, and march and dance music. Golden Records also has a set of Bible stories often told to children. They are dramatized in narrative voice and song. Additional recordings you will want to consider are:

American Folk Songs for Children by Pete Seeger. (FC 7601, Folkways).

Counting Games and Rhythms. (7056, Folkways).

Give Your Child a Head Start by Shari Lewis. (Camden).

It's a Small World. (Disneyland Records).

Boys Choir. (Disneyland Records).

Learning the ABC's and How to Count by Rosemary Rice. (Columbia).

Poems for the Very Young by Marni Nixon. (CL 16, Bowmar).

Rhythms of Childhood. (FC 7653, Folkways).

The Three Little Pigs by Boris Karloff. (TC 1129, Caedmon).

Walt Disney Songs. (HL 9503, Columbia).

Another way to develop attentive listening skills is to read aloud to your child. This might be done at a regular time each day, such as late afternoon or at bedtime. Let your child choose the stories he likes and do not hesitate to reread a story that he knows and loves. Children take a particular delight in hearing their favorite stories over and over. Holding your child close while you read to him is in itself a pleasant experience. Some children will begin to recognize words during these reading sessions and will be on their way to reading. Those children who do learn to read easily are often the same ones who have been read to by their parents, older siblings, grandparents, and others close to them.

When your child sees you reading he often has a desire to do the same thing. Let him know that you go to books, magazines, and newspapers for information and enjoyment. Allow your child to discover that reading enables a person to do things like bake a cake, play games, put something together, and so forth.

Take an interest in your child's questions. Don't let him feel that his questions are foolish or stupid. Help him understand that you also wonder about many things. Encourage your child to express himself orally by letting him tell about his experiences with his playmates. The environment which you help to provide at home sets the stage for learning how to read at school.

Your child's home environment will greatly affect his future life. You can help him to become confident by giving him responsibilities. He should dress himself and see to it that his belongings are kept in their proper place. When he accomplishes a difficult task or has made something, he will enjoy recognition.

An active alert child also needs to have playthings to manipulate and experiment with. Let him play with blocks, paints and crayons, clay, scissors, and scrap materials. Give him an old alarm clock to take apart to find out what makes it tick. These are some of the simple everyday experiences that can build a child's self-confidence.

Questions and Answers

My child starts school in September. What can I do to set him on the right path? The best thing you can do is to encourage your child to look forward to a new and gratifying experience.

Tell him about his teacher and the new friends he will make. Explain to him that there are many new things he will learn and do. Most children are eager to start school and this enthusiasm should be kindled.

My child learned to walk and talk early. Does this mean that he will learn to read quickly? There is no hard-and-fast rule that children who are early talkers will be early readers. Generally, however, this is the case. The child who talks early usually catches on fast in reading. He knows many words and has excellent language ability.

On the other hand, a child who learns to talk late may not necessarily be backward or retarded. In fact, many late talkers have average or better than average intelligence. Sometimes a child experiences an emotional block which holds him back from learning to talk. In some families late talking seems to be a hereditary factor. Therefore late talkers are not necessarily late readers.

If, however, the child is a late talker because of intelligence factors, he will of course be slow in learning to read.

Should I teach my child the alphabet? A child's initial instruction in learning to read is facilitated if he knows the names of the letters of the alphabet and if he can print them. It is not necessary to teach the alphabet in sequence, and you should not attempt to give formal instruction. Some specific suggestions for working with your child on the alphabet are given in Chapter 5. Some of the suggestions presented will also help your child to learn the sounds of the alphabet.

Are prereading experiences ever disadvantageous to a child entering the first grade? Children benefit from the enrichment of prereading activity. Not all children get the experience they need prior to entering the first grade and these are children for whom the reading readiness program has been designed. The only time prereading experience is a disadvantage is when a teacher does not recognize the readiness of a child whose home background has in fact successfully provided that experience. It is possible for a child to waste time in first grade going through readiness experiences in which he is already skilled. Generally teachers are able to diagnose which children are ready for beginning instruction in reading. Readiness comprises a multiplicity of developmental factors, and a weakness in only one or two factors would not mean that the child is not ready to read. That is why modern teaching requires a degree of individualization of instruction. Teaching that focuses on the average or below average child might cause the better prepared child to make insufficient progress and become an underachiever. The parent-teacher conference helps the teacher to assess a child's maturational skills and readiness for reading instruction.

Chapter 4

How Your Child Learns to Read

The process of learning to read is tied in with the total complex of reading skills. In Chapter 2 we considered the dynamic process of reading. By way of definition, reading is a process whereby the individual makes meaningful interpretations of verbal symbols. As a child develops he learns to listen and to communicate orally. Reading is an extension of oral communication. In learning to read the child must interpret the printed symbols and learn that these symbols stand for speech. When he is able to say the words represented by the printed marks he is said to be reading. Whether he says the words out loud or to himself, he must say them correctly.

When the child says the correct words they fall into place in a logical sequence of ideas which he interprets. The meaning is easily recognized by the child because of his facility in comprehending speech. If he leaves words out, or if he doesn't recognize enough of the words, he cannot get the meaning from the sentences. If his recognition is too slow he cannot get meaningful sequences. In order to read effectively the flow of words must closely approximate the speech that he hears. Only then will his reading be able to convey the correct meaning.

We may say that the first step in learning to read is the discovery that printed words "talk." As the child continues to develop and increase his reading ability his word-recognition skills expand. As he matures his recognition of common words becomes faster and more accurate. Many words which he recognizes instantly are called sight words. More details on the development of a basic sight vocabulary are presented in Chapter 5. In time the child develops a sight vocabulary of several hundred words. From this basic vocabulary emerges word-attack skills which the child uses in figuring out new words. He no longer has to be told each new word, for he is able to sound it out. It eventually becomes unnecessary to read aloud and the child learns to read silently.

As proficiency in reading skills continues the child begins to move into areas beyond his experiences. Through reading he is introduced to more complex sentence structure, unfamiliar vocabulary, and ideas. Getting meaning from the printed page becomes increasingly difficult. In order to keep up with these complex skills the child's vocabulary must increase. He must learn many new words, ideas, and concepts.

The child continues to discover different types of reading. At school he is helped to read a variety of materials. He learns that he must satisfy different needs and purposes in reading. He learns the difference between reading for pleasure and reading to study new concepts. He may read to find out how to build a model airplane or how to bake a cake. Gradually the higher level reading skills require the child to make inferences, draw conclusions, note main ideas and supporting details, locate information, note sequence of events, and derive meaning from higher levels of vocabulary.

At this point reading becomes reflective and evaluative, an active process whereby the reader reacts to what is read. He does not accept everything stated just because it happens to be in print. A good reader is a critical reader constantly making judgments on the author's presentation.

In brief, then, the child learns to read by initially responding appropriately to the printed words. He learns to equate the printed symbols with speech and he responds intellectually and emotionally. He brings into play his reasoning skills and employs then as a part of the total reading process. As he develops proficiency he learns to adjust to a wide variety of reading, from recreational to study material. Reading becomes a dynamic process which encompasses a complex of skills.

Although we can study the process of reading and break it up into its constituent parts, review its nature and how it is learned, we must bear in mind that all children are different. Because one teaching technique works for most children does not mean that it will be effective with all children. In order to determine the effectiveness of a procedure we need to observe how it works when used with a particular child. If the child exhibits a high level of anxiety, or if he is resentful or bored, these factors could lead to a dislike for reading. If on the other hand the child responds well and seems to enjoy the experience, puts forth an effort and derives satisfaction, then the method is effective for that child.

The important point to remember in how children learn to read is that they learn at different ages and at different rates. In Chapter 3 we considered the factors involved in reading readiness. All children are not ready to begin reading instruction simply because they are chronologically ready to be in the first grade.

As a parent you should be aware of several specifics regarding your role in how your child learns to read. First it must be stated that the parent's role in helping a child learn how to read is complex. Some children respond exceedingly well to parental help. Others experience frustration and failure. What is it that seems to make the difference? Quite often success depends on how the child views the help the parents try to give. If he feels the help he is getting stems from love rather than a sense of duty, the chances for success are greater. When parents demonstrate their interest in reading by reading themselves, this habit may well be picked up by the child.

As parents you must demonstrate a sensitivity toward your child's feelings. How does he feel about being deprived of his play time in order to study? Does he feel he is not able to meet your expectations of his achievements at school? Your sensitivity to these realities will help you to determine your role in any given situation. The main thrust of your help should be in providing suitable reading material. Let your child have books that are easy and interesting for him. Don't insist that he read only his school books. It is through reading a wide variety of books that your child's vocabulary will grow, and this will help him to develop language fluency.

Ultimately your child learns to read through a variety of methods. If he is happy in his learning then the procedure is good. If he becomes frustrated or anxious the method is bad for him.

In the following chapters you will learn about the various teaching techniques in reading used in the elementary and secondary schools,' and what you can do to reinforce these techniques at home.

Questions and Answers

How do I know if my child is doing his best at school, and whether or not I should put pressure on him? This is a very difficult question because of the complexities involved. Much depends on the child's maturity for his particular grade level. There may be a number of conditions that could prevent a child from doing his best. For example, what is his physical condition? Does he have a great deal of energy or does he tire easily? Does he appear to learn rapidly or is he a slow learner? What about his school history? Did he have difficulty with beginning reading instruction? How does he view himself? Does he exhibit hostility toward learning? The answers to these questions should give you an idea of what may be contributing to your child's poor work. Your child's teacher may also be helpful to you in this matter since he has undoubtedly made many observations of your child's behavior in a classroom setting. The teacher's observations coupled with your own may provide some clues as to how you should proceed. In any event putting pressure on the child would probably not improve matters.

PART II

Reading
in the
Elementary School

Chapter 5

Reading in the Primary Grades

Think back to your own school days for a moment. If someone were to ask you the question, "How did you learn to read?" would you be able to present an adequate answer? Do you actually remember how you learned to read? Chances are the process was so natural you were not even aware of the complexities of the task. This is because learning to read is a natural process. In fact reading is so natural that it is unusual for one not to develop the skills involved, if he has adequate teaching.

Most people are unable to describe the method whereby they learned to read. It is interesting to speculate on this point. Why is it so difficult to spell out an exact method of teaching reading? Undoubtedly because teaching is more of an art than an exact science.

The methods by which children learn to read are varied and complex. Many youngsters are able to recognize whole words on sight without being fully aware of the components of the words. They see the Shell Oil sign or the Texaco star and are able to make the associations. Somewhere along the line they are able to read the words without the accompanying symbols.

In an age of billboards, traffic signs, a booming publication industry, radio, and television, is it possible that a child cannot learn to read? Is a child who has a reading problem just plain stupid? This is not usually the case. Let's consider the major factors in the teaching of reading at the elementary school.

How Are Children Taught to Read?

In an attempt to find solutions to reading problems some people have advocated a particular method as a panacea or cure-all. These individuals have criticized instruction by stating that phonics is not taught in the schools. They state that this is the only method whereby children can learn to read adequately. This point needs to be considered. Certainly the teaching of phonics is one of several word-recognition skills, but does it constitute a complete educational program of reading instruction?

We will spend some time with this issue since it has been of such vital interest to everyone. First however, it will be helpful to develop some understanding relative to the initial stages in the process of learning to read.

Reading Readiness

Should you be concerned if your child does not bring home a reading book on the first day of school? The answer is no. Chances are it will take the teacher several weeks to determine which children are ready to read. What is meant by reading readiness? By what methods does the teacher determine who is ready and who isn't? Is reading readiness a valid program or does it simply waste the child's time? You will certainly want the answer to the question, "Is my child ready to read, and if not, why not?"

First let's consider the psychology behind the readiness program. Reading is considered a developmental task, one that a child begins to accomplish when he is ready for it and not before that time. If you have more than one child you are already aware of various differences in their development. Perhaps Susan learned to walk at ten months but Harry took his first step several months earlier or later. Learning to walk is a developmental task. The child will walk when he is physically ready and able to do so. Apparently no amount of prodding or help will speed up this process.

Speech is also a developmental task. A baby will learn to talk when he is ready. There is no set pattern whereby all children will learn to utter their first words at six months. Since reading is a developmental task it follows that all children will not learn to read automatically because they have reached six years of age and are arbitrarily placed in the first grade.

The same holds true for those children who are ready to read before the age of six. No doubt you have met youngsters who can recognize the alphabet or read from a primer long before entering the first grade. Bear in mind that admission to the first grade is contingent upon age alone and not ability or readiness.

The normal or above average child usually has had enough prereading experience and is ready for primer work as soon as he enters the first grade. Children who have not had adequate preschool experiences or who are not mentally mature generally need the readiness exercises essential in preventing initial failure in reading.

Judging Reading Readiness

How does Johnny's teacher determine whether he has achieved readiness for reading? There are certain standardized tests which may be used. The Metropolitan Reading Readiness test published by the World Book Company is one test used in schools throughout the country. However, no test can tell us everything about a child. It can only give us indications of strengths and weaknesses and no parent or teacher should emphasize the results of a single test. In addition to tests the teacher must also use a method of systematic observation to determine reading readiness in a child.

As a parent you may not be able to view your child as objectively as an outsider. You may rationalize and tend to minimize certain inadequacies and deficiencies. A good teacher is vitally interested in the education of his students. If your child has such a teacher, this teacher will attempt to make some observations. As an intelligent parent you will be able to make similar observations along the lines of the following:

Attention Span

Does your child have an adequate attention span? That is, can he sit long enough to pay attention and listen? Or is he restless and easily distracted?

Attending doesn't just happen. It has to be learned and this learning begins in infancy. Parents influence this process through the type of physical environment they provide. The child's interpersonal relationships with parents, peers, and others are also factors which influence his learning to attend. You can help your child to learn to pay attention by providing him with opportunities to practice this behavior. A child will learn to pay attention through a one-to-one relationship with a parent who listens and responds by explaining, interpreting, and clarifying. Children without a reasonable attention span when they enter the first grade lack the readiness to learn.

Motivation

Is your child sufficiently motivated? Does he have a desire to learn to read? Teachers are quick to recognize that most youngsters are extremely eager to learn to read. Such a desire is usually developed at home especially during the preschool years. Your own attitudes toward reading and school will do much to foster this important desire to learn. Without this desire children are not ready to learn.

We may ask "How does a child become motivated?" In the early years the child is motivated because he wants to please his parents and his teacher. He wants attention and praise. Positive responses by the parents and the teacher are strong motivators for the child. You can play an active role in motivating your child. When you pay attention to what your child is doing, you communicate your interest and pleasure to him. When you answer his questions and encourage him to explore and make discoveries, you help to develop and sustain his motivation.

Personality

Is your child outgoing? Is he confident in his abilities? Is he independent, resourceful, and cooperative? These positive characteristics facilitate the learning process. Look for these characteristics in your child. If he possesses them this is a good sign that he has a readiness for reading.

Physical Adroitness

Have you had your child's vision and hearing checked? Can he distinguish differences in sounds and forms? Can he interpret pictures? These characteristics are important in learning to read, and a deficiency here could result in a reading retardation. How about your child's motor coordination? Is he in control of his body as he moves about? Does he exhibit proper coordination as he runs, jumps, and skips? Does he have lots of energy? These physical factors also indicate readiness.

Mental Abilities

Does your child have adequate mental abilities for his age? Can he follow simple directions, use words properly, recite children's poems, or repeat a story he has heard in proper sequence? It is very difficult for parents to assess their child's mental abilities for a particular age. The teacher evaluates mental abilities through standardized tests. If you believe that your child lacks sufficient mental maturity, the teacher can test him and discuss the results with you. If there are deficiencies they will affect the child's readiness for reading.

Language Factors

Does your child speak clearly in sentences? Can he figure out the missing word of a sentence if it is suggested by the context? Is he able to recognize words beginning with the same sound? Can he recognize the letters of the alphabet? All of these language factors must be developed before a child can learn to read.

The child's thought processes are dependent upon his language abilities. Through language he expresses himself, makes judgments, sees relationships, and recalls learning experiences. Some of the games and activities suggested in this chapter will facilitate the development of those linguistic abilities necessary in learning to read.

Visit Your School

It would be wise for you to contact your child's teacher within six to eight weeks after the start of the first-grade year. At this time the teacher will have made the necessary observations and have your child involved in a learning program. Those students who rank high on standardized tests and teacher observations are provided a beginning program of reading instruction. Children who are low in the language factors previously mentioned are provided with necessary prereading experiences. When sufficient progress is shown in these areas the child will most likely experience success in his initial attempts at learning to read.

Visiting the teacher has additional value at this time because he will be able to reveal his observations to you. He might have noticed any hearing or visual deficiencies, and can also indicate to you information regarding your child's readiness and place in the class. The teacher will undoubtedly be able to give you additional insight regarding your child's associations with others. On the other hand you are in a position to help the teacher to gain insights into your child regarding his home experience, specific abilities, and individual characteristics. In the final analysis, no one knows a child better than his parents do. Therefore, a meeting with the first-grade teacher will have far-reaching effects and benefits for your child.

How to Help
Your Child Achieve Reading Readiness

There are numerous factors involved in the complex state of readiness for reading. Readiness is developed in a variety of natural ways. Part of it comes about as a result of the child's normal development. Children learn to speak effectively and to distinguish between objects they see and the words they hear as a result of their experiences in the family and with friends and play groups. These factors are so natural that they are not significantly influenced by actual teaching.

However, in situations where prereading experiences have not been sufficient, parents can help to provide more of them. What can you do to help your child along these lines if such help is indicated as necessary? The interest you show in your child's activities is most important. In our hectic age it is not always possible to afford our children the time and interest they deserve. However, some of the most simple situations can increase the trust, love, and respect that exist between parent and child. These situations can provide the very activities necessary for learning to read.

You can help your child to develop an interest in reading and a desire to learn to read by continuing to read to him those poems and stories which you know he enjoys. Tell him that he will one day learn to read such stories independently. Take advantage of those opportunities which require your child to think and to express himself. On automobile trips let him read the road signs and encourage him to associate the shape of the sign with the words and their meanings. Examples are *stop, yield, railroad,* and so forth.

While you are working around the house or yard let your child help you by giving him simple directions to follow. Comment on his activities, for instance, "How nicely you are coloring that picture!" "Perhaps your friend Johnny would like to see your model automobiles." In this manner your child learns to associate words with objects and to increase his understanding of concepts.

Prereading Games

Take advantage of opportunities to play games of an educational nature with your child. Such games should be in the spirit of play.

Sentence Completion

A game which most children enjoy involves sentence completion. You might say, "Alan, I'm going to tell you something but I will leave the last word out. You try to guess what it is." You should then proceed with a sentence such as:

"I shall wear my heavy overcoat today because the weather is _____."

The child may answer, "cold," "freezing," "bad." Any answer that makes sense is acceptable. This activity helps to develop the ability to get word meanings from context. The child learns to develop an understanding of the various shades of meaning which words have. This is a basic word-recognition skill which your child will need in his initial steps in learning to read.

Recognizing Initial Consonants

Another game involves practice in recognizing the beginning sounds of words. This game is strictly oral. It does not involve writing the letters in a notebook or on a slate. Say to the child, "I am going to the department store to buy _____."
Then begin to mention articles with the same initial consonant sound such as *radio, rings, rake,* and so on. Have the child think of other items having the same initial sound.

Collect objects and pictures. Ask the child to select those items that begin with an *m* or a *d* sound. Your child may recognize sounds in words but may not understand what you mean by beginning sounds. He can learn this through repetition of words such as *meat, milk,* and *mustard,* and *desk, day, and doll.* You can vary the exercise by saying, "See if you can catch the word that does not begin with the same sound as the others. Listen—*dog, door, top.*" This game helps the child to distinguish initial sounds and thereby increases his auditory discrimination. As a related activity you and your child might look through an illustrated magazine to find pictures of objects with similar beginning sounds. These could be cut out and pasted in a scrapbook. One or more pages in the scrapbook could be devoted to each initial consonant. The child could add to this from time to time.

Related activities should be devised for words with similar ending such as *boy* and *toy,* or *might, right,* and *light.*

Recognizing Letters of the Alphabet

The ability to recognize the letters of the alphabet is an important prereading experience. Alphabet blocks and the ever present *"A is for Apple"* book provide initial contacts with the alphabet. It should be noted that it is not necessary to teach the alphabet in sequence. The child begins to recognize the various letter shapes as you teach him. He can check on his learning by playing a sort of bingo game. Print different letters on a cardboard square. As you call out certain letters have the child cover them up with a piece of cardboard. This process takes time and requires patience. If the child is a slow learner he should not be forced or rushed. A slow learner should be taught one or two letters at a time.

The necessity of reading readiness cannot be minimized, as it is such an important factor in the program of reading instruction. Children vary in their language ability, vocabulary, and interest in reading. Their hearing and seeing abilities also vary. Because of these factors, children's needs differ in relation to responses to printed words and to reading readiness activities. Where some children have already begun to read before entering the first grade, others are just about ready to begin instruction and still others are not ready.

The reading readiness program at your child's school is not designed to hold back those students who have started to read on their own. Similarly it should not prevent instruction for those who would benefit immediately. Those reading readiness activities that are in the program will not be unnecessarily prolonged. The readiness program will help those children who are mentally immature, physically handicapped, slow in perception, or whose native language is not English.

Phonics Versus the Look-Say Method

In the past decade certain critics of education have created a controversy based on the false premise that the teaching of reading can only be accomplished by a single method— either the look-say (sight words) or phonics. A great deal of confusion has resulted in the public mind as a result of this controversy.

Books have been published advocating a return to phonics as a single method of instruction. The authors of these books have denounced public education as having shortchanged today's youth by ignoring phonics and pushing the look-say method. Other people have taken an opposite stand and advocate that the look-say method is the only approach to teaching children to read. Is it possible that the teaching and learning of reading, constituting a complex of skills, can be reduced to the utter simplicity of one method? This seems highly unlikely.

Let's examine the facts about what is being taught in the public schools today. In the first place our public schools are not using the look-say method as an exclusive approach. Nor have they rejected the teaching of phonics. Reading specialists and authorities in the field are generally agreed that the teaching of reading cannot be accomplished through the exclusive use of the look-say method. Obviously such an approach would require the memorization of innumerable words, rendering the method impossible and therefore ineffective.

Phonics is considered an important word-recognition skill. Through phonics the child is helped to identify printed words which he has not seen before. He must also understand the meanings which the word represents. A lack of phonics in the reading program could weaken a child's chances of becoming a strong efficient reader.

You are justified in asking why some reading instruction, no matter what the method, fails. The answer lies in the fact that many school systems have a staff which is at least one-third inexperienced teachers, poor library facilities, crowded classrooms, and a poor public attitude, both moral and financial.

In the booklet "Learning to Read," published by Educational Testing Service, Princeton, New Jersey, a group of nationally recognized reading experts state,

> Reading is indeed a complex process; and because reading has so many facets, the teaching of reading is also complex. No single device, such as phonics or sight words, can reach across the range of skills that an efficient reader uses. We are agreed that there is no single best way of teaching children to read. Wise reading teachers make appropriate use of all the tools and techniques available at the time most suitable for using them. They do not speak of *the* method of teaching reading because they understand that teaching reading is a composite procedure that assembles and uses the best methods that professional theory, research, and the practical common sense of competent teachers have been able to devise.

Skills in Word Recognition

As children begin the process of learning to read, most teachers introduce a few printed words which are common to their vocabularies. The children are then able to recognize these words when they see them again. These few words are used as a base to enable the children to read simple sentences of two or three words almost immediately. It should be emphasized that these few words are common and simple. They are not learned as a list but rather one by one. The teacher introduces them carefully and selects them from conversation in class.

This procedure of introducing a few initial words does not constitute a tremendous feat. On the contrary it is part of a composite approach whereby a child learns to recognize and identify printed words. This is the so-called look-say approach which some critics insist has been used exclusively to the neglect of phonics.

As your child learns these few beginning words he is using the skills which will enable him to figure out other words which he will soon encounter in his daily reading. These are the word-recognition skills of which phonics is an essential element.

When your child enters the first grade he will recognize several thousand words as he hears them spoken and he will know their meanings. What he probably will not know are the relationships between sounds and the letters which represent them. Here is where phonics enters the picture. So many parents are concerned about phonics as a result of the reading controversy, yet how many of them are able to distinguish the difference between *phonics* and *phonetics*? Can you?

Phonetics is the science of speech sounds. An international phonetic alphabet has been designed to represent each of the sounds of speech. This alphabet is very different from our own. Many college speech and communications courses teach the phonetic alphabet, which may be used to express the sounds of any language. Phonics on the other hand is a simplified form of phonetics and is used in the teaching of reading and spelling.

Since children entering the first grade already know both the sound and meaning of thousands of words, these are tied together in phonics. The child must learn to relate the letters in the printed word to the sounds in the spoken word. With English as complicated as it is (most letters have a variety of sounds) this is no small task.

As your child begins to relate sounds to letters in words he is using phonics. This skill enables him to sound out a word which he has not seen in print before. If the word is already a part of his speaking vocabulary he will know the meaning. Phonics per se will not help the child to get the meaning; other skills such as contextual clues are used here. However, in the initial stages of learning to read, unfamiliar words are not introduced in the basal reading texts used in schools. These texts utilize a controlled vocabulary made up of words which are encountered frequently in the book. Some critics have complained that this makes for a dull and boring approach. It should be noted, however, that the children are not restricted to the basal reader. Most classrooms have supplementary reading materials in which the vocabulary is not so carefully controlled. The school library offers many beginning reading books for children.

In phonics the child associates sounds with letters. In sounding out words the child is able to pronounce them. If the word is a part of his speaking vocabulary the sound of the word recalls the meaning to him. By sounding *d* he gets a clue to the word *dad*. By sounding *sp* in *spell* he has a clue to the pronunciation of *speak, spank,* and *split*. Children need to be taught the sounds of letters as they appear in words. Teaching the sounds of separate letters will not do. Consider the double vowel sound ŏŏ as in *lŏŏk, bŏŏk,* and *gŏŏd*. If the child is taught this sound in isolation, what happens when he comes across words such as *sōōthe, smōōth, sōōn,* and *tōōth?* The child should be taught to recognize new words as they occur in his reading. This motivates him to learn the word-recognition skills. When a child encounters a new word his phonic skills can only provide him with pronunciation and not with word meaning. Since the purpose of reading is to get meaning and not merely to call out words, good teachers unite phonics instruction with instruction in the word-recognition skills.

Since the actual teaching of speech sounds is such a complicated process it should only be assumed by those trained in the teaching profession. Both you and your child are apt to face frustration if you attempt to do this teaching yourself.

As an informed parent you should know the basic facts about phonics and other related word-recognition skills. It has been generally agreed that there are two types of word-recognition skills—phonics, and meaning through context. Let's consider these further. In phonics the child responds to the sounds represented by the letters in the word, and by parts of words such as syllables, prefixes, suffixes, and roots. Recognition of word parts is spoken of as *structural analysis*. In meaning through context the child recognizes words by clues provided by the other words in the sentence. These skills are not used in isolation. Children are taught to utilize them simultaneously in actual reading.

As the child develops facility in the use of the word-recognition skills he learns to recognize words instantly. He no longer needs to analyze a word after he has encountered it once or twice. For instance, the word *mother* is soon recognized instantly as a whole because of the position of the letters in it. As adults we do not have to figure out words each time we meet them; we recognize them as wholes. Children also learn to do this. The process is much quicker with youngsters who are mentally mature.

If a school is going to administer an effective reading program it must include the word-recognition skills of which phonics is only one part. Other word-recognition skills include structural analysis (recognizing prefixes, suffixes, roots, and other familiar parts of compound words), syllabication, and the use of the dictionary.

If your child is to be successful in his phonics instruction, he should have the following: an interest in reading, a knowledge of a small number of familiar sight words, the ability to distinguish similarities and differences in word sounds, and knowledge of the alphabet. Although some critics would disagree, a child should learn this sound-letter association through sight words instead of starting with isolated letter sounds and trying to build these sounds into words. The number of sight words may range from fifty to five hundred. This beginning program should be taught regularly and systematically as the child progresses through the primary grades.

Difficulties and Problems
in the Teaching of Phonics

Can you imagine how tedious and boring it would be if you had to sound out every letter combination in every word you read? Analyze your own approach to reading. How often must you stop to figure out a word? Do you look at every letter in a word? Certainly not. You get the word instantly from its configuration and a few letter clues. This makes for smooth efficient reading.

The exclusive use of phonics that has been advocated by some educational critics could lead to the development of word-callers and extremely slow readers. The word-caller quite often is only interested in pronouncing words and consequently gets little meaning from the printed page. Since reading involves getting the meaning the word-caller is not actually reading. The exclusive use of phonic drills can result in boredom and loss of interest in the story. Prolonged drills in phonics lack the thrill of reading a story and can cause children to approach reading very slowly. For example, a fifteen-year-old boy who still reads at the primer level was coached for years in sounding out words. His initial reading problem is unknown at this time. However, after years of phonics drills he must sound out practically every word in his primer. After a half hour on one page he begins to guess at words because he tires of the process which requires him to sound out each word. He has virtually no sight vocabulary. Bear in mind that this is an unusual case and is mentioned here for illustrative purposes only.

The difficulties in teaching phonics are almost self-evident. Unlike some other systems, English is not a phonetic language. Educational studies have been conducted to show that Mexican children rarely have reading problems. In fact, the Mexican child is usually three years ahead of his American contemporaries in reading. This is due primarily to the fact that Spanish is a phonetic language; there is practically a one-to-one relation between letters and sounds. This of course makes it easier to learn to read.

In English we use twenty-six letters but have at least forty-four separate sounds. Some letters have two or more sounds. For example, the letter *a* carries some twenty-two sounds. The sound of the long $\bar{a}$ in *mate, date,* and *relate* may be spelled out in six different ways. Or, observe the following example:

> *ea* as in *bear*
> *ei* as in *their*
> *ai* as in *stairs*
> *ay* as in *gray*
> *ey* as in *they*
> *e* as in *there*

You can readily see the difficulties a child might encounter if he has learned the pronunciation of *ea* as in *bear* and comes across words such as *read, heard, hearth, smear, ear, fear, tear, beard.*

The sounds of letter combinations should be taught as they appear in words and not in isolation. In checking his pronunciation of an unknown word the child must check to determine whether the word makes sense in the sentence. This word-recognition skill is an important part of the phonetic approach.

How Is Phonics Taught in the Schools?

When the child has a few basic sight words he can begin to recognize the various letter-sounds. Phonics instruction usually begins with those consonants which almost always have the same sound. These are *b, d, f, h, j, k, l, m, n, p, r, t, v, w,* and *z.* These sounds are best taught as the initial sounds of short familiar words. They should not be taught in isolation. In teaching the sound of *t* for instance, the teacher will give the words *tell, take,* and *talk,* and ask for others having the same beginning sound. This process is continued with all of the other initial consonants. Since these consonants are combined with the vowel sounds—*a, e, i, o, u,* and *y*—these too are introduced early in the program. As the child progresses the sequence is continued with instruction in the common word endings such as *s, ed,* and *ing.*

Through this instruction the child builds up his letter-sound associations during his first year at school. The second year he begins to learn the more difficult consonant blends, such as *bl, ch, cl, fl, fr, sh, sl, st, th,* and *tr.* He also learns the various vowel combinations, such as *ai, ay, ea, ee, ie, oa,* and *oi.* He may learn some of the variant sounds of *a* and of *o* when followed by *w* or *o.*

Moving to the third year the child gets a great deal of experience in using all of the letter-sound associations he has learned. Much emphasis is placed on consonant blends, vowel combinations, and speech sounds. Rules for pronunciation are derived. An example is the changing of a short vowel sound to a long one by the addition of a final *e* as in the following:

pan — pane
bit — bite
dot — dote
cut — cute

After studying double vowel combinations in words such as *meat, play, boat,* and *sleep,* the teacher will help the children to conclude that "When two vowels go walking, the first one does the talking." It must be recognized, however, that there are always exceptions to the rules.

Other Primary Reading Skills

As your child proceeds with his reading experiences in the first three grades he will begin to develop a wide range of skills. He will develop the ability to read longer and more complex materials. His vocabulary will grow both in reading and in conversation and writing. His comprehension will be increased as he reads longer, more difficult passages. In the early grades he will also learn to use the dictionary independently.

Just how does the school enable your child to develop these skills? There are essentially three types of materials that the teacher will employ to help your child to develop these skills. They are:

The Basal Reader—This reader is carefully constructed and contains a controlled vocabulary so that new words are introduced in easy doses.

Textbooks—These are written on a wide variety of subjects.

They generally go far beyond the basal readers and the vocabulary is not as carefully controlled.

Books for Enjoyment—The school library has many interesting books for children. You can help your child to increase his enjoyment by providing him with his own copies of books, and by taking him to the public library to browse and to borrow books.

In using these three basic types of materials the teacher strives to help each child to develop the word skills and comprehension skills basic to reading. Instruction in the primary grades has as its goal the mastery of those skills whereby children can attack and acquire new words and grow in their comprehension skills.

Approaches to the Teaching of Reading

The Basal Reader Approach

Any discussion of how reading is taught in the schools must include the basal reader approach, since this method is so widely used throughout the country. The basal program is a series of books graded in difficulty in linguistic approach and content. Many basal reading series cover the entire elementary school years from prereading and reading readiness activities through beginning reading and on up to grade six.

The basal reader is intended to serve as the core of material used in the teaching of reading. Basal readers are planned around a carefully controlled vocabulary. New words are introduced as the child progresses through the reader and learning is reinforced through repetition of words introduced. Actually the entire approach utilizing a controlled vocabulary and varied content has not changed appreciably since the days of the McGuffey Readers in the 1830s.

Most series begin with a *soft-covered* readiness book. The beginning reading materials, also paperback, are called preprimers, and there are usually three of them. The reading readiness book usually contains only pictures, such as a boy and a girl, mother and father, and a dog and cat. The preprimers contain just a few basic words used to introduce the child to reading. These words may be Tom, Susan, baby, mother, father, up, down, jump, and so forth. These materials are followed by a primer which is usually identified as 1^1 on the cover of the book. This is intended for use during the early part of the year. As the child progresses he moves to the "First Reader" identified as 1^2. This completes the material for the first grade. These are usually followed by two second-grade and two third-grade readers. There are separate readers for grades four, five, and six.

Accompanying these readers are consumable workbooks. The child uses the workbooks to reinforce the material of the readers. He responds to his workbook by writing in its pages, following the printed directions or the directions of the teacher.

The basal reading series provides a wealth of related materials for the teacher to use in planning the reading lessons. These materials include Dittomasters to be duplicated in the school, large printed cards for group work, and small cards for individual work. These cards contain various phonic elements, words, and phrases. There are paperback supplementary story books using the controlled vocabulary of the basal readers. Finally, there are films, filmstrips, records, tapes, and illustrations and photographs correlated to the basal readers.

The teacher derives his methodology through the use of a manual which accompanies each book. The manuals are comprehensive and contain detailed lesson plans for every selection. They constitute an extensive handbook on how to use the basal readers.

In general the content for the first-grade reader centers around a family comprised of a mother, father, a first-grade girl and boy, a baby, a dog, and a cat. This one-family theme is sometimes dropped by the end of the primer. Some series are based on urban settings and multiethnic characters to keep within the actual experiences of the children taught. The content of recently published basal readers is quite varied, with stories about space travel, animals, folk heroes, and adventure, as well as poetry and nonfiction.

The basal reading lesson is typically developed in three clearly defined steps: (1) preparation, (2) reading the story, and (3) follow-up activities. The first step is intended to prepare the child for the story. There are three main phases in preparation. The first phase is motivation; the teacher employs techniques to arouse the child's interest in the story. He may present a film-strip or recording or use some other attention-getting device to stimulate discussion and develop the child's enthusiasm. The second phase is concerned with the presentation of ideas, concepts, and facts which may not be familiar to the child and so need clarification. The third phase is known as preteaching of vocabulary. During this phase the new words are presented. Most basal reading programs rely heavily on the look-say method, although some stress phonics during this phase of the lesson.

The second step in the lesson is reading the story. This involves a method of guided reading and rereading. The teacher leads the discussion by asking a question about the title. "What do you suppose this story is about?" "What does the title tell you?" "What's happening in this picture?" "What do you think will happen?" The children are then directed to read silently to find the answers. The first silent reading of the story is followed by discussion. Then there is oral rereading of the selection. The children may be asked to reread the sad, happy, or funny parts of the story, to describe the feelings of the characters, to find the sequence of events in the selection, or engage in other types of activities designed to develop thought processes, meaning, and vocabulary.

The final step in a basal reading lesson is the follow-up activity. There are two types of follow-up activities. One involves skill development and the other a variety of enrichment activities. Phonics plays a major role in skill development. The teacher uses those techniques previously described for the teaching of phonics. Other word-recognition techniques such as structural analysis and context clues are also used. The workbooks provide for development in a variety of skills and are assigned after the reading and rereading activities. It is during this part of the lesson that the teacher is able to individualize instruction by working with children individually and in small groups, emphasizing those skills in which the children need the most help. The teacher may also read related supplementary selections, play records and tapes, use jingles and rhymes, and if children are able to do some independent reading, make assignments from supplementary readings.

Although the basal reading series is rich in phonics and word-recognition skill development, the class size and the wide variety of individual needs sometimes make it very difficult for the teacher to incorporate all aspects of the lesson plans.

The Language-Experience Approach

In the language-experience approach the children are motivated by the teacher to express their thoughts, ideas, and feelings about a particular experience. Perhaps the class has gone on a field trip to the zoo, the farm, or the market. The approach is valuable in that it incorporates the unique interests and needs of each child. The first step to reading becomes one in which the experiences of the child are utilized in print, rather than selecting books written by an adult. Through this method interest is virtually guaranteed. The teacher draws a story from each child and may then record them with a primary (large type) typewriter, or they may be written on experience charts large enough for the entire class to see. This insures that each story is an artistic expression of a child. In reading his own story the child is helped by the teacher to write and spell some of the basic words. He later progresses by writing his own captions and stories. During this process the teacher demonstrates the relationships between sounds and letters, and the child proceeds at his own pace. This provides a degree of individualization of instruction. This method is not used as an exclusive approach. It requires a great deal of planning on the part of the teacher. The various phonic skills are developed through the vocabulary of the language-experience themes. The approach is informal and not very well systematized. As the children develop proficiency in reading they usually progress to a basal reading series.

The Phonics Approach

We have detailed the importance of phonics and have indicated the scope and sequence involved in the teaching of phonics. Some mention of phonics as a teaching approach is necessary at this point. By and large most phonics materials have been used to supplement the basal readers. However, some schools have decided that they want an earlier introduction of phonics and a more intensive type of instruction in this area. Most phonics materials stress the phoneme-grapheme relationships (the sounds represented by letters and letter groups), and the rules of phonics, to which there are exceptions. Some materials emphasize a synthetic procedure of sounding and blending, while others utilize a word-to-sounds method as used in the basal readers. Phonics programs tend to emphasize word recognition through the application of phonics rules and the learning of the phonemic equivalents of letters and letter groups.

Special phonics programs have been designed to replace the basal readers but have not done so. In most instances these programs are not used exclusively but as supplements to other approaches.

The Linguistics Approach

The linguistics approach is based on the following premises: (1) children should first be taught the letters of the alphabet by name, not by sound, (2) beginning reading vocabulary should only include words in which each letter represents only one phonetic value, and (3) words with silent letters or less common sounds should not be introduced. This leaves a beginning reading vocabulary of mostly three-letter words with a pattern of consonant-vowel-consonant, and all short vowel sounds, such as "Nat the rat sat by the fat cat." Several basal reading series have been developed employing the linguistics approach. They all follow the principle that the decoding of words is the most important objective of the reading program. Decoding refers to the translation of printed forms into their spoken equivalents.

The Phonetic-Alphabet Approach

Since many words in English are not written phonetically, a number of problems arise in the teaching of reading. That is why the use of phonics cannot stand alone as a method of learning to read. There does exist an International Phonetic Alphabet in which each special character always represents a particular speech sound. This alphabet can be used to express the sounds of any language. From time to time efforts have been made to produce a special alphabet for the English language that would be phonetically regular so that each letter symbol would always represent the same sound.

In the early 1960s Sir James Pitman developed the Initial Teaching Alphabet. His idea was to employ a regularly phonetic alphabet to teach beginning reading. He based his idea on the premise that learning to read is easier and more quickly accomplished with an invariable correspondence of symbol and sound. His alphabet, known as i/t/a, does not represent a method of instruction. It is an alphabet that can be used to teach beginning reading. The i/t/a consists of a separate symbol for each of forty-seven consonant and vowel sounds. The capitals are the same as lower case only larger. Most of the present letters are retained, with new characters designed to facilitate the transition to traditional orthography. There are still unanswered questions as to the desirability of using a transitional alphabet.

Wide publicity has been given recently to another alphabet system known as *Words in Color*. In this system the sound-symbol relationship is provided through the use of colors. The forty-seven consonant and vowel sounds are each represented by a particular hue. Various spellings representing a particular phoneme are all printed in the same color. As the child begins to use this method the main cue is the color rather than the grapheme (letters and letter sounds). Needless to say, children with color vision defects and poor auditory perception have difficulty with this method.

The Programmed Learning Approach

A programmed approach is one that begins with very easy material and builds up in steps to more complex work. One cannot proceed to the next step until he achieves mastery of the level he is working on. Such programs provide immediate reinforcement of learning, are self-pacing, and are completely individualized.

The use of the computer for programmed instruction in reading is in its initial stages of development. The computer has numerous advantages in that instruction may begin at the child's instructional level, the amount of time allotted to each child varies so that children can work at their own pace, the computer serves as a strong motivating factor for children, and it can handle a wide variety of instructional materials that are carefully programmed and sequenced.

These various approaches to reading instruction have been described so that you may have a richer understanding of the techniques employed in teaching children to read. No one approach is exclusively employed by the schools. Rather the overall approach is eclectic, bringing to boys and girls a wide variety of learning modalities.

Reading in the first three grades provides the foundation for later reading instruction. At the end of the third grade the child should have a large sight vocabulary, words he recognizes instantly. He should be able to sound out many new words and be able to read orally with fluency and intonation. His silent reading of third-grade materials should reflect adequate comprehension. He should be able to read a wide variety of easy materials.

Games to Help Your Child in Phonics

If the teacher indicates to you that your child is experiencing some difficulty in phonics he may suggest ways in which you can help at home. The games and exercises described here are offered as a guide. As a parent you are too close to your child and therefore limited in the kinds of instruction you can administer successfully. But you can help by showing your interest and enthusiasm. Do not prolong the games and exercises. Utilize them as often and as long as your child's interest is high and he asks for more.

Matching Consonants and Word Endings

This game may be used to provide help in learning sounds or parts of words:

b	all	ell
f		
t		
w		
sm		

Print the column of letters on the left on a sheet of paper or cardboard. Move the sheet up or down to match with various word endings such as *all*, *ell*, and other combinations.

Associating Letters and Sounds

This game is used to give help on initial consonants, blends, and rhyming words.

Construct a baseball diamond on a sheet of oak tag or cardboard. Each player tries for a home run by providing a word for each of the three letters which are placed on the diamond, such as *play*, *sail*, *take*, and *home*. You can vary the game by placing words around the diamond. Each player must then think of a word that rhymes with each of the words on the bases.

The Word Wheel

By using oak tag or cardboard you can construct word wheels. These wheels will provide your child with short, concentrated drill practice in learning consonant blends such as the following: *br, ch, cl, dr, fl, fr, gr, pl, sh, sp, st, th, tr,* and *wh*.

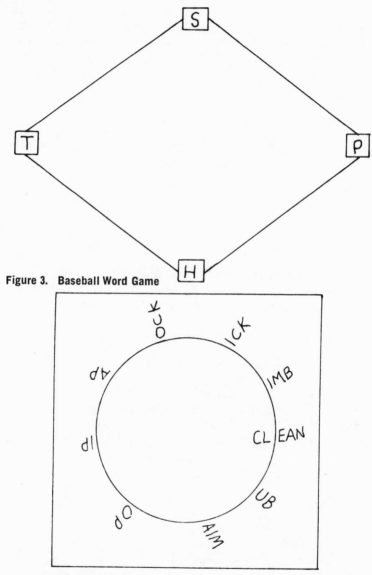

Figure 3. Baseball Word Game

Figure 4. Word Wheel

The Treasure Hunt

Collect objects and pictures to be placed in a bag or small carton. Have your child close his eyes and draw out one of the objects. Then have him look through a stack of printed 3″ x 5″ cards to find the word that correctly names the object.

Fishing for Words

As a variation of the above game, prepare a set of folded cards held closed by a paper clip. Place the cards in a bowl. Have your child fish out the cards with a fishing rod consisting of a small magnet suspended from a piece of string. He may keep only the fish he can read. He returns the others. The words you print on the cards should come from the child's basic reader.

Bingo

This word game is relatively simple to construct since it uses words instead of numbers. Children in the second and third grades can have a great time with this game. Using words from your child's basal reader, construct 5″ x 7″ word bingo cards containing twenty-five squares. That is five squares under each letter of BINGO. Print a word in each square. Make several such cards so that two or more can play. Of course no two cards should always contain the same words in the same squares. Then make a master deck containing all the words appearing on the 5″ x 7″ word bingo cards. Prepare pieces of oak tag or cardboard small enough to cover up one square. As you call the words from the master deck after shuffling, the child uses the oak tags to cover up the corresponding squares on his bingo card. When he covers up a row directly or diagonally (in either direction) across his bingo card he wins the game. If two or more are playing the first one to cover up a complete row is the winner. All players should read their words aloud at the conclusion of each game. A variation would be to continue the game until the entire card is covered. In the case of two or more players, the first one to completely cover the card calls bingo and declares himself the winner.

Your role as a parent during the first three years of grade school is to help your child get ready to read, to share his enthusiasm in his initial attempts to read, to be patient and understanding, to cooperate with the school, to help your child in any way the teacher suggests, and to provide him with plenty of books and a home environment conducive to learning and growth.

More Word Games

Following are some additional word games that are fun to play. These games have been suggested by the National Reading Center (Washington, D.C.) as being appropriate for children who are just beginning to read—first to third graders. They may also be used with older children who are experiencing difficulty in learning to read. The Center publishes many pamphlets and brochures to help inform all citizens about reading issues and to promote national functional literacy.

Alphabet Game

Purpose: To practice beginning sounds and spelling words.

Materials: On twenty-six small squares of heavy paper or cardboard (1½" x 2"), print the letters of the alphabet, plus several extra squares for each of the vowels.

Procedure: Two or more can play. Mix up the letter cards and place them face down on a table. Each player in turn draws a square and has ten seconds in which to call out a word that begins with that letter. Otherwise the card is returned to the pile. When all the cards have been drawn each player spreads his letters in front of him and uses them to spell as many words as he can. The consonant letters may be used in only one word, but vowel cards may be reused. Children should be given any help they may need with spelling. To score, allow one point for each letter card won during drawing, and one point for each word completed and correctly spelled. The player with the most points wins.

Variations:
1. Increase the number of letter cards so that more words can be spelled.
2. Make cards with letter combinations such as *bl, br, cl, cr, pl, sl, st, tr, ch, sh, th, ph.*

Ten Pins

Purpose: To practice word recognition and word sounds.

Materials: Ten circles, about 1½" in diameter, cut from a piece of colored paper. Staple them through the middle on a large piece of heavy paper or cardboard so that they form a triangle (like bowling pins set up in an alley). On each circle print a different word that has caused the child trouble. On each of ten small cards (½" x 1") print one of the words which appear on the colored circles. On the paper beneath each circle write a single number (1-10).

Procedure: Two or more can play. Place the small cards face down on the table. Each player in turn selects one and places it under the colored circle which contains the same word. Each player must say the word to get credit. Score is determined by the number under the circle, and the winner is the one with the highest score after all cards have been placed.

Variations:
1. The number of circles used may be increased so that there are more words.
2. Different categories of words can be put on different colored circles (words that look alike on green, words that begin with the same letter on red, and so on).
3. Short phrases can be printed on the circles.

Partnership Reading

Purpose: To stimulate interest in reading, to motivate and improve skill in reading aloud, and to emphasize reading as a shared activity with an adult reading model.

Materials: Books from the library or from the child's home collection of favorites.

Procedure: There are several ways to conduct this activity. The child selects a book that appeals to him, either one that he has never seen before or one that he knows well and likes. It should be one that he can read with relative ease and satisfaction. He can determine this by reading a paragraph or two. In one variation the adult reads a sentence from the story aloud after which the child reads the same sentence aloud. Since the adult has just read the sentence the child may have less trouble pronouncing words and will have the satisfaction of reading with greater fluency than usual.

In another variation adult and child take turns reading every alternate sentence orally. Although the child still has the example of the adult's reading he will not have heard the sentence that he reads.

Still another highly motivational variation is for the adult to choose a book, pick an especially exciting chapter, read it aloud to a high point in the story, and then leave the child to continue to read independently. If the adult has chosen well and the relationship between adult and child is a close one of shared interest and mutual respect, this technique works well. It can be particularly effective with children who are already quite good readers, usually eight years and older.

Partnership story writing can be fun too, to emphasize the relationship between writing and reading, to provide practice in reading, and to stretch the child's imagination and his ability to describe his experiences and feelings in words. Let the child select a subject that interests him, such as baseball, ghosts, playing with friends, or things he would like to do. The child dictates slowly and watches as the adult prints each word exactly as the child says it. Each story should be reasonably short, not more than five or six sentences. First the adult reads back to the child what he has written. Then the child reads the story aloud. Each story can be saved to be continued or combined with others to develop into a book or diary. The child should be encouraged to read his stories to other adults and to his friends. Since his own words have been used to prepare his reading material, the words and language patterns will be familiar and give him greater confidence than would other material not based on his own spoken language.

Questions and Answers

How can I find out about my own child's reading? As a parent you are in a position to learn a great deal about your child's interests. Frequently these interests are pursued in reading. What kinds of stories does your child enjoy? What stories seem interesting to him? Listen to him when he reads aloud. Does he experience difficulty with common short words? Do the longer words seem to give him trouble? Is he able to figure out unfamiliar words? Does he use the word-recognition skills described in this chapter? Does he enjoy reading in his free time? The answers to these questions will provide you with important clues about your child's reading.

What can I do to help correct the faults in my child's reading? Through listening and observation you can detect some of the common faults in reading. You can indicate to your child that it is not necessary to point his finger at the words, or to move his head from side to side. If he persists at this it may be an indication of poor eye muscle coordination, although this is not always true. Some children like to use a card as a place finder in the early stages of reading. This is considered a helpful technique. During silent reading your child's lips should not move. This is a type of vocalization that is not necessary and may lead to a slow reading rate later on.

You can help your child to correct these faults indirectly. If you keep pointing them out it may strain your relationship and do more harm than good. For instance, if a word is mispronounced the best thing you can do is to pronounce it correctly. But do not stop the child at that point. Unless he asks for help, let him finish the sentence or idea being expressed. Do not let him get the impression that you are looking for mistakes. Encourage your child to read aloud, be a good listener, and try to appreciate the passage or story. By being attentive and interested you will be able to reach your child when it becomes necessary to make corrections or offer assistance.

Should I give my child lessons in reading? You should not attempt to give your child formal lessons in reading. Do not attempt to teach him from a basal reader or textbook, or to follow the instructions in a teacher's manual. In short, the job of instruction belongs to the school. You can help to enrich the school's program by giving your child the kind of practice and play suggested by the games and activities described in this chapter. Steer clear of long tedious drills, and make sure that you praise your child for any progress he makes.

How can I determine what progress my child is making? Since reading is a long sequential process you can check on your child's progress through observation and contact with the school. Ask yourself these questions: Does your child show an interest in reading? Does he understand what he reads? Is he able to relate a story in sequence? As he comes to the end of the first grade is he able to do some independent reading?

During the early grades the teacher may use standardized tests, such as the reading readiness test mentioned in this chapter. Through observation and testing the teacher can evaluate the child's progress. At any rate, contact with the teacher will help to keep you informed of your child's progress.

Why is my child not learning to read? Usually a child learns to read when he is ready. Pushing and prodding during the initial stages of instruction will only tend to make matters worse. You can help by providing your child with plenty of easy and interesting books. He is more likely to respond in a relaxed type of environment.

If, however, your child shows severe incompetence in learning to read, you will need help from the school in determining the causes and in taking a specific plan of action to correct the situation.

How and why are children grouped for instruction in reading?

Children are placed in reading groups in an effort to help them to make the most progress possible for them.

The reasons for this are fairly obvious. Not all children learn at the same rate. It is easier and better for a teacher to work with a limited range of reading ability, rather than a wide range.

Within such groups the poor or slow reader is not frustrated by the superior reader. At the same time the good reader is able to move ahead while the poor reader gets the help so essential to his overall growth in the development of reading skills. Grouping readers according to ability helps *all* children to learn to read better. Of course it should be noted that in any grouping arrangement the sensitivity of the teacher toward his pupils is of paramount importance. He must constantly be aware of the needs of each child in each group. Through his sensitivity he allows each child to work at his own pace using materials of appropriate interest but at the child's instructional level. He must work to minimize any stigma attached to a slower group. Also it should be pointed out that the grouping is dynamic and changes periodically according to needs. The groups do not work together exclusively throughout the day but only during certain periods of time allocated by the teacher for specific instruction. The understanding teacher lets all his pupils know that he expects them to do their best at all tasks. Children grouped together for reading may be grouped differently for arithmetic and other instructional and play-time activities.

My child's school has a program of "Individualized Reading Instruction." What does this mean? It has long been recognized that the individual differences of children require individualized attention. Through testing and other diagnostic techniques the reading skills of children are assessed. On the basis of skills achieved, each child works on materials specifically prepared to develop and increase those skills needed. Usually this type of program is conducted in a reading laboratory. In such a laboratory, each child may be working on a different task and each at his own rate of learning.

Chapter 6

Reading
in the
Intermediate Grades

The intermediate school program comprises instruction in grades four, five, and six. During these years children receive reading instruction representing a continuum of their earlier learning experiences in the primary grades. At this time there is a broadening scope of reading activity, called developmental reading skills.

Developmental reading is primarily concerned with the continuing improvement of those skills acquired at the primary levels. To achieve this refinement of the reading process most schools employ the basal readers. There was a time when basal readers were no longer employed after the third grade. However, their usefulness at the higher levels has been demonstrated. Although there are many supplementary readers and other reading materials used, the basal readers serve as the primary focus of instruction. Typically, the intermediate readers contain a wide variety of reading experiences, including stories and nonfiction which have generally been adapted to specific reading levels from higher level articles and literature. One popular basal reader has stories about animals, inventions, young Americans, the sea, and treasure hunting.

As we described in the previous chapter, each basal reader is accompanied by a workbook. The children write in these paperback books, answering questions, following directions, spelling, and so forth. The workbooks are helpful to the teacher in planning small group instruction. The teacher's manuals, containing suggestions for instruction, are not as detailed as are the ones used in the primary grades. This is because instruction in beginning reading is so very complex. Once the basic skills are developed in the primary grades, the teacher is ready to provide experiences that will reinforce and expand those earlier skills and his task will become less complex.

From the fourth to sixth grades you should expect that your child will increase his basic sight vocabulary, develop superior skills in word recognition and analysis, and broaden his reading scope. In the area of structural analysis of words he should be able to recognize many new words by dividing them into syllables. At this level a child who tries to sound out a word letter by letter rather than by syllables needs special instruction. You may further expect your child to become more skilled in figuring out word meanings through context. As your child progresses through the grades he will become less dependent on phonics clues in figuring out word meaning.

During this time the child will also be taught the higher level skills such as reading charts, tables, graphs, maps, pictures, and symbols. He will be presented with textbooks in various subjects, as well as specially written newspapers, magazines, and informational books such as encyclopedias. Textbooks are not carefully graded in difficulty as are the basal readers with their controlled vocabularies. Therefore it becomes increasingly important for the child to adapt his general reading skills to the specific requirements of his textbooks. He will receive instruction in developing reading techniques in such subject areas as social studies and science. The special techniques required in textbook reading call for skills in locating information such as specific facts or dates, organizing (perhaps in sequence) and summarizing material, making inferences, and drawing conclusions. Through the development of these skills the child's interests are broadened and he now enjoys reading for pleasure.

As he enters the intermediate grades he should have developed sufficient basic reading skills to enable him to read independently and widely. If he has not developed these skills, or even if he is deficient in just a few of them, it is likely that difficulties will be encountered in his effort to read the higher level materials. In fact, if the intermediate materials are too difficult for the child he is said to be at his "frustration level" in reading. This means that he cannot recognize enough words to get adequate meaning from the passage he is reading.

There are a number of factors which may influence your child's reading development. At about age ten the child's eyes reach adult size. This means that he can read for longer periods of time without eye strain or fatigue. He can recognize similarities and differences more readily and can therefore associate sounds and letters and distinguish word configuration with greater ease. An increased maturity of the brain and nervous system enables the child to learn more rapidly, and indeed he does so during these years. The more knowledge the child acquires the more comprehension he gets from his reading. In the act of reading, the child brings his total experience and background to the printed page. The more he knows the more his reading comprehension is facilitated.

Reading Interests

A wide range of reading interest should be encouraged by providing plenty of books at home. Trips to the library should be as frequent as possible and the child should have his own library card. At school he should be encouraged to use the school library. Many classrooms have book and magazine collections for use during reading periods right in class. Here are some suggestions for activities at home:

- You can help your preadolescent child by encouraging

him to read independently and voluntarily. The more he reads during these years the greater are his chances to enrich his vocabulary, build his knowledge of the world about him, and enhance his facility and enjoyment of reading.

One of the best ways for parents to encourage their child in reading is to work through interests. Johnny was a model airplane enthusiast and needed information on building and flying them. His father bought him a book and a couple of popular magazines to provide the information Johnny needed. Susan checked out a library book on sea shells to help her identify specimens from her collection. Janice was so interested in reading about the stars that she asked her mother to buy her a telescope, because, she said, "I want to study the universe." Jimmy began reading sports magazines because he could find out about the players on his favorite team.

• Have your child share his interests with you. Ask him to select an article from the daily newspaper or a periodical which interests him and discuss the article with him. Ask him questions about it to see how well he grasps the main idea and see if he can recognize the supporting details. Help him to follow the sequence and to draw conclusions about what he is reading. Newspapers and popular magazines are an excellent resource to stimulate interests and discussion.

• Help your child to improve his comprehension skills through informal discussions of those books which you have both read. Discuss those points which will demonstrate whether or not he has recognized the central thought. You should vary your questions according to your child's needs and abilities. If you find that he has difficulty identifying the central thought or main idea, ask him to recall some of the supporting facts. From these facts you can then lead him to the main idea.

• Provide your child with plenty of books that appeal to him. Don't hesitate to allow him the freedom to select the books he likes. As he reads them let him make his own interpretations of what they are about. He will enjoy sharing his ideas with you and this will help him to understand the world in which he lives.

Games to Play

Following are some games that are suitable for children in the intermediate grades. They can also be used for fast learning third graders, and slower learners in grades seven through nine. These games have been tried and tested and are fun to play. They will greatly facilitate your child's learning of new words and spelling.

Word Categories (*two or more players*)

In this game each player makes up a list of ten or more categories (for example, tools, fabrics, fruits, vegetables, household items, furniture, and so forth). The players then write down as many items as they can for each category within a ten-minute period. One point is scored for each correct item and the player with the most items is the winner.

As a variation to develop deeper concentration for the players, a single letter is agreed upon by all. Then each item written for each category must begin with the same letter. Again the player who writes the most items in a given time is the winner.

Compound Words (*two or more players*)

This game will help your child to see how compound words are formed from two smaller words. It will also give him practice in the use of the dictionary when he needs to find out whether a particular compound word is spelled as one word, with a hyphen, or as two separate words. It will also help him with his spelling.

The first player begins the game by calling out two words that form a compound, such as *highway*. The next player's task is to form a new word from the last element of the compound *highway*. He can say *wayside*. The next player may say *sidewalk*, and so the game goes (*walkway, waylay, layman, manpower, powerplant, plant food, food chain,* and so forth). The game continues until a player cannot think of a compound word to be formed from the last element of the preceding player's word. He is then out of the game. The last remaining player is the winner.

Word Rummy (three or more players)

This is an absorbing game that is designed to improve vocabulary through an understanding of prefixes, suffixes, and root words. Following is a list of root words and affixes from which more than eighty words may be formed. Using 3"x5" index cards, prepare the following deck of seventy-four cards: *Prefixes*: seven of *re*, four of *un*, three of *pre*, two of *mis*, and two of *dis*. *Root Words*: three each of *finish, heat, view, call, tell, spell, cover, even, understand, claim, taken, form, written,* and *trust. Suffixes*: five each of *ing, ed,* and *er*.

The dealer shuffles the cards and deals out six to each player. The remaining cards are placed in a pack face down on the table. The object of the game is to build words from the cards in hand. The players must try to put as many words together from the affixes and roots which have been dealt to them. As in rummy, each player draws a card from the pack when his turn comes up. He may discard any card that he cannot use. When a player scores twenty or more points he may call "rummy." All the players then count up their points accordingly:

For calling rummy	—	five points
For prefix and root (e.g., *review*)	—	ten points
For root and suffix (e.g., *called*)	—	ten points
For prefix, root, and suffix (e.g., *unfinished*)	—	twenty points

The winner deals the next round. A player needs 225 points to win the game.

The Scrambled Sentence (one or more players)

This game will help your child to put words together to form sentences. Select some sentences from your child's textbook, or use a well-known slogan or saying. Using 3"x5" index cards write each word in the sentence on a separate card. Make a duplicate set for each player. Each set should be shuffled to scramble the sentence. The first player to construct the sentence wins the game.

Questions and Answers

I'm confused about my child's reading test scores. What do they mean? Parents frequently ask this question as they are concerned about how well their child is reading. Unfortunately any attempt to measure the reading ability of a child is at best an estimate. All that the test can do is to give a general idea of a child's reading level. If your child's reading level is reported to be 3.3, it really doesn't mean much to you unless you have some understanding as to how the score is determined. Reading levels are usually indefinite. A child's reading level may be identified with how well he reads a particular book, in many schools a basal reader. The basal readers are graded in difficulty from beginning reading to the more advanced levels. If a child reads from a fifth-grade reader with adequate comprehension he is identified as reading at that level. Children are expected to progress through the series at the rate of one grade level per year, or one basal reader per year.

There are essentially two types of reading tests used in the schools. They are known as informal and formal tests. The informal test helps the teacher to determine the child's reading level by having him "try out" in the various levels of basal readers. When a book closely corresponds to the knowledge of words the child has, as well as his understanding of ideas, it may be concluded that the child is reading at the particular level of the book. The next highest level would be too difficult for him until he develops the skills necessary for that level. The information yielded by the informal reading test helps the teacher in planning instruction for the child. Since the test is administered on an individual basis—one child at a time—the teacher is able to get additional clues regarding the child's reading performance. The informal test yields diagnostic information needed by the teacher in order to individualize instruction.

A formal test is one that is published commercially and generally administered on a group basis to the whole class. Such a test yields a score that is computed by comparing the child's performance with the scores of many children who have previously taken the test. If your child's reading score is reported as 3.3, it means that he scores as well as an average child who took the same test in the third month of the third grade. Since this test, known as a formal standardized test, has limitations, the score can only be interpreted as an estimate of the child's reading skill. The major limitation of the test is that it is merely a comparison with other children taking it.

Another important consideration is the range of ability which a child demonstrates. This range may be as great as one year. For example, a child who scores 3.5 on any particular day may score anywhere from 2.5 to 4.5 at another time. This is why test scores may vary so much from one week to another. There are a variety of reasons for this performance. If a child is tested when he is hungry, tired, or emotionally upset, his performance may be affected. Therefore test scores are merely estimates of a child's reading ability. They should not be considered as a precise measurement.

I believe my child needs professional help on reading outside of school. What should I do? First you must determine the kind of help your child needs, and if he would benefit from outside help. Your best approach here is to consult with your child's teacher, principal, or the school's reading specialist. They will be in a position to provide you with sound advice. You will need to answer such questions as, "Does my child need help to supplement, replace, or reinforce the school program?" You also need to consider whether or not there is a problem that could be corrected by outside help. After consulting with school officials and concluding that outside help would be valuable, you should ask for recommendations from the school. They may be able to suggest a nearby university clinic that specializes in helping children with reading disabilities. The university clinic would be able to diagnose and pinpoint specific problem areas. They also provide specific instruction to overcome the diagnosed weaknesses. A reputable tutor or private remedial service would also be able to provide intensive individual instruction if this is needed.

What relationship, if any, exists between reading and spelling? In the act of reading the child must recognize words from which he derives meanings. When he encounters unfamiliar words he must decode them. That is, he associates the printed word with the speech it represents. In spelling, on the other hand, the child has to encode. That is, he thinks of the letters that represent the sounds of the words he is spelling. The average reader generally recognizes whole words on sight and does not need to look at each letter. For this reason an individual may be an efficient reader but a poor speller. Poor readers who have difficulty with word recognition are rarely good spellers. Therefore a close relationship does exist between efficiency in reading and success in spelling.

The fact that English words are not always written the way they sound causes trouble for young spellers. For example, many children tend to spell words phonetically—*nite, nife, coff, laff,* and so forth.

In beginning reading instruction, the teaching technique used most often is the introduction of whole words. In spelling instruction the child first learns to write by copying before he knows the sound elements and their letter representations. The teacher first uses the word to be spelled in a sentence, then by itself, and then writes the word on the chalkboard. The word is then analyzed by breaking it into its constituent parts. The child's attention is directed to the letters. Syllables are then separated by vertical lines. The teacher reinforces the learning process by introducing various sensory impressions; for example, the children are asked to pronounce the word, to trace the letters in the air, to spell in unison, and finally to write the word from memory.

Good spelling therefore is based on the correct perception of the word followed by repetition and other sensory techniques so that the speller remembers how the word is written. The techniques used in word recognition parallel those in spelling (for example, syllabication, analysis, sense appeal). When a child learns how to spell a word from memory he can read that word without difficulty. Learning to read and spell are fairly complementary processes and success or difficulty in both are often related.

My child is not reading up to his grade level, yet his teacher promoted him to the next grade. Shouldn't a child be retained if his reading is not up to par? It depends to a degree on the child's mental, emotional, and physical development. Often a physically mature child will feel very much out of place in a class of younger children. The emotional impact on the child may be so impressive that it could offset any value that might be gained through retention. On the other hand a child's physical and emotional development may be such that retention would produce beneficial results.

Many schools have curricula designed to take care of individual differences in learning. Therefore a child could function adequately at the next grade level even though he is not thoroughly prepared to read grade level materials. The matter of retention should be carefully considered by the school officials and the parents involved to insure that any action taken is in the best interests of the child.

My child likes to read comic books. Won't this hamper his progress in reading? Probably not. Comics are written in the vernacular and may in fact introduce many new words into the reading vocabulary of the child. Many experts agree that instruction in reading should rely heavily on a child's interests. If he is interested in comic books he should not be discouraged. Parents can help by providing other materials in addition to the comics. This will help to broaden the child's reading interests. He needs to find out that other materials can be as interesting if not more fun to read than comics. As his reading ability increases and matures he will tend to read fewer comic books.

PART III

Reading
in the
Secondary School

Chapter 7

The Adolescent Years

This chapter presents an overview of the reading skills taught during the adolescent years. The development of reading skills does not stop at the elementary grades but continues into the secondary schools. Reading instruction in grades seven through twelve represents the development of the higher level skills. This instruction builds upon the skills developed in the intermediate grades and provides for a continuum of experiences at the secondary levels.

Vocabulary Development

The teenager's vocabulary is an important area of growth and continues to be developed at the secondary level. Specific instruction must be given to enable the student to broaden his vocabulary. At this stage the young adolescent develops precision in the meanings of words. He must realize that many words have more than one meaning. For example, the word *record* has several meanings depending upon the context: Let's look at the *record*; John holds the *record* in high school track; Have you heard the latest rock *record*? The teacher must *record* all grades on a special form. Through this type of presentation the adolescent becomes acquainted with multiple meanings. He also learns figurative language and idiomatic expressions such as "breaking the ice," "facing the music," and so forth.

In writing it becomes necessary for the adolescent to be able to call to mind various words needed in order to adequately express his ideas. Instruction in vocabulary development includes an understanding of connotation and denotation. The adolescent learns that the denotation of a word is the literal meaning, while the connotation is the interpretive meaning. As instruction in vocabulary proceeds through the higher grades students are taught that they can learn new words through several areas of approach.

The first area of approach to word meaning is through context. The student is asked to read the entire sentence to see if he can figure out the meaning of an unfamiliar word through the surrounding clues. If this fails the next step is known as structural analysis. Here the student tries to figure out the word through his knowledge of prefixes, suffixes, and root words. Instruction is given in learning the meanings of common affixes and also Latin and Greek roots. If structural analysis does not help, the student is referred to the dictionary. To use the dictionary effectively the student must develop alphabetization skills, understand the guide words, understand the various dictionary symbols—the breve, the macron, the circumflex, and the tilde—work out the pronunciation of words, identify the accent of words, understand the derivation of words, and identify the part of speech of a word. Finally he must be able to use the dictionary to learn the various meanings of words.

Following are some suggestions you may present to your teenager to help him to increase his vocabulary during his junior and senior high school years:

• Keep a vocabulary notebook, or create a set of 3" x 5" cards. On one side of each card write the word only and on the other side write the word and its meaning. Use the word in a sentence.

- Study the words in context.
- Break each word into its basic elements—root, prefix, and suffix. In the case of a compound word break it into its simple words.
- Associate the root word with its synonyms and antonyms.
- Use your new words in writing and in speech.
- Study the technical vocabulary of your various school subjects.

Some further suggestions will help to increase vocabulary through reading. Following is a specific systematic approach to vocabulary improvement for your teenager.

When you come to a strange word:

1. *Check it and skip it.* Put a little check mark ($\sqrt{}$) over any word you do not recognize by sight. Then go on and see if you can understand the meaning of the sentence without it. You can often learn the meaning of the word by noting its context.

2. *Break it up.* If number 1 doesn't work, try to take the word apart. Guess all you can from the parts you recognize; it may be enough for the purpose you have in reading.

3. *Sound it out.* If numbers 1 and 2 fail, pronounce the word softly, to the best of your ability. This is often very helpful.

4. *Look it up.* If you must know the word to understand what you're reading, and if numbers 1, 2, and 3 don't work, reach for the dictionary. Here is where your vocabulary can grow by leaps and bounds. In order that the first three steps may work better next time you use the system, open the dictionary to the word and then carefully and thoughtfully:

   a. Pronounce it correctly.
   b. Study its origin, roots, prefixes, and suffixes.
   c. Read all the meanings of the word.
   d. Write the word down on your vocabulary list.

Comprehension Skills

Reading comprehension continues to develop through the adolescent years. Comprehension becomes increasingly important as the teenager begins to delve into subject matter much more vigorously than he did during the elementary school years. Comprehension in reading involves a multiplicity of factors all of which must be dealt with in grades seven through twelve. As a parent it is important for you to know about the kinds of reading skills that need to be developed during these crucial years.

Comprehension involves the understanding of the printed page. Full meaning cannot always be conveyed by a single word and the efficient reader must learn to interpret words in their contextual setting. Words are comprehended as parts of sentences, sentences as parts of paragraphs, and paragraphs as parts of complete writings. The following factors comprise the total act of reading comprehension:

- the ability to associate meaning with the printed symbols
- the ability to react to the sensory images suggested by words (visual, auditory, and so forth)
- The ability to interpret the proper denotations and connotations of words
- the ability to understand words in context
- the ability to understand the phrase, clause, sentence, paragraph, and total selection
- the ability to select the main idea of a passage
- the ability to recognize supporting details
- the ability to note sequence and organization of a passage
- the ability to follow directions
- the ability to see relationships: part-whole, cause-effect, and so forth
- the ability to interpret figurative language
- the ability to make inferences and draw conclusions
- the ability to read critically, to identify the author's intent, purpose, mood, and tone
- the ability to recognize various propaganda techniques

- the ability to recognize facts and opinions, or judgments
- the ability to react to what is read

All of these skills must be taught throughout the secondary grades; they cannot be expected to develop automatically. It is the school's responsibility to provide specific instruction to insure that all pupils will develop their reading potentials to the fullest extent. Ideally all teachers at the secondary level are teachers of reading. Each is responsible for the development of reading skills in his particular discipline. In practice this does not always work. Therefore, some students might find themselves in need of special reading instruction at the secondary level. Special reading programs are usually available in the junior and senior high schools and will be discussed later.

One of the most important comprehension skills is the recognition of the main idea of an article or chapter, as well as the main idea of each paragraph. Students are taught that the main idea is usually stated in the opening sentence, or the topic sentence. The sentences that follow present details to support the main idea. Secondary students need to be very aware of main ideas and supporting details particularly in regard to the reading they do while studying. In developing this skill, various passages with the main idea stated in the first sentence are presented to the student. Variations in paragraph structure are introduced to demonstrate other organizational approaches to writing. A paragraph may be organized with the topic sentence at the end. In this case the supporting details would be presented first and then the topic sentence would complete the paragraph. Students might also learn that the main idea may be stated in the middle of a paragraph. Additionally, there are rare organizational patterns in which each sentence in a paragraph carries equal significance.

Here are some suggestions that you may use with your teenager to help him to find the main idea:

- Have the youngster read a short selection and make up a suitable title.
- Have him read the title of a short paragraph, essay or

chapter. Ask him to predict what the material will be about.

• Have him read the introduction of a chapter noting what the author has outlined.

• Have him read the summary or concluding paragraph of a chapter and tell in one sentence what the chapter covered.

• Have him read a paragraph and then state the main idea in one sentence.

At school, your teenager is taught to identify the main idea. Sometimes a paragraph does not have a single sentence that summarizes the main idea. Therefore, the student is taught to infer the main idea based on the sentences in the paragraph. Making inferences and drawing conclusions are also important comprehension skills. These skills are sometimes referred to as reading between the lines.

Another comprehension skill is reading for organization. The student must be able to see the relationship between the main and subordinate ideas so that he can arrange these in logical order. He should be able to use a variety of materials from various sources and to make inferences and draw conclusions. He should be able to comprehend organizational patterns with regard to time sequence, contrast, and cause-effect relationships. Additionally he should be able to summarize what he has read. Summaries are of particular benefit in reading literature, essays, and social science materials. They are also important for the study type of reading to be discussed later.

You can help your youngster to develop summarizing skills by using the following techniques:

1. Have your teenager summarize a message so that it would be suitable for a telegram. Have him use only ten words to get the message across.

2. Tell him a story or relate an interesting event and ask him to write a brief summary.

3. Have him summarize materials from a variety of sources.

4. Ask him to write newspaper headlines from paragraphs which you present to him.

The reader with efficient comprehension skills is a critical reader. Such a reader is not passive and does not accept everything simply because it happens to be in print. He actively responds to what he reads. He reads with a questioning attitude. Who is the author? What are his qualifications? What is his purpose in writing? Does he want me to believe something? Why does he want me to believe it? It is this searching, probing attitude that results in critical reading, a comprehension skill that must be taught and developed for efficient reading comprehension.

Skills Used in Studying

We cannot leave the area of reading comprehension and critical reading without looking at the skills used in studying. These skills become increasingly important to secondary students as they prepare for their future.

You can help your teenager in his studies by familiarizing him with one of the most successful study techniques developed in education. The technique was developed by Professor Francis Robinson and is based on how people learn and remember. It is called the SQ3R study formula. The following is a description of the technique prepared for secondary school pupils.

S Stands for Survey

In the study formula the *S* stands for *survey*, sometimes called prereading. The survey phase of the study method enables you to select what you should know.

In making a survey of a textbook chapter, first consider the title. The title is a generalization intended to cover the topic under discussion. It prepares your mind for the material at hand and it should help you to guess something about the contents. Then review what you already know about the subject. Your comprehension and retention will improve if you learn new material in the context of previous knowledge.

A quick reading of the chapter will help you understand the author's organization, tempo, and style; it will suggest to you what the author is trying to do. If you are studying a complete book, thumb through it. Take a look at the table of contents and try to get the feel of the book as a whole. Take notice of the charts, tables, graphs, and illustrations. Try to determine the author's purpose. Is he describing something? Is he trying to prove or explain something? Is he presenting facts or opinions? The survey helps you establish your purpose in reading.

Q Stands for Question

The second phase of a good study method enables you to understand ideas rapidly. Here is where the *Q* or *Question* part of the formula comes in. What questions would you like the chapter to answer? Jot these down. Be specific with your questions. They will help you to understand the material and to fix ideas in your memory. Use the old journalistic formula of *who, what, when, where, why,* and *how?*

Three R's—Read, Review, Recite

Next we come to the three *R's* in the formula. R_1 refers to *read*. In reading a chapter, essay, or article, study the first paragraph or introductory statement. In a book read the preface or foreword. Usually the author tells you in his introductory remarks what he plans to develop. When you finish reading the first paragraph read the closing paragraph or concluding statement to get a summary of generalizations and conclusions. Then read the entire chapter, focusing on the generalizations and supporting details. Concentrate on any examples, illustrations, or references. This technique of reading the first and last paragraphs and then the complete text constitutes a plan of detailed reading.

When your detailed reading is complete and you have been able to fix the main ideas in your mind, you are ready for the next step in the study method. R_2 refers to *review*, a process of relearning. Your review will be most valuable if you concentrate on building a well-organized structure of the topics in question, emphasizing main ideas and principles, understanding relationships between ideas, making proper inferences, and drawing logical conclusions.

Keep in mind also the following aids: the table of contents; chapter titles, headings, and subheadings; introductory and concluding paragraphs; questions which you have raised as well as those at the end of the chapter; topic sentences; key words and phrases; italics and boldface type.

The final step in the study method is R_3, or *recite*. At this point close the book and try to recall the material you have read.

The last two parts of the SQ3R study formula, review and recite, may be repeated as often as necessary until the material is learned. You should review your studies often.

The study method described here is not easy. Study per se is not something that can be rushed. These are not shortcuts to be substituted for hard work. This study method will help you learn in an organized, systematic way. Initially this method is time-consuming. However, you can make any modifications necessary for your own study needs. You have the framework for a logical system of study based on the way you learn and your job is to make the system work.

The ability to study well is a key to successful mental preparation for exams. Remember the five essential steps: (1) Survey, (2) Question, (3) Read, (4) Review, (5) Recite.

In addition to reading for study and the development of a logical study technique, the adolescent learner must develop proficiency in interpreting charts, maps, tables, and graphs. These pictorial devices are often used in textual materials to enhance comprehension of the subject. Specific instruction in this area is provided at the secondary level, usually by teachers of the specific subject matter.

The teenager is faced with departmentalized studies at the secondary levels. Each of the content areas in which he studies requires all of the skills mentioned in this chapter as well as those skills needed for reading in the respective content areas. We will turn now to the more common content areas to see just what the specific skills are. These are the skills that are taught within the various disciplines. All of the content areas require special vocabulary and comprehension skills.

Reading in Mathematics, Science, and the Social Sciences

The vocabulary skills in mathematics require that the student learn and recognize those terms that are special to the discipline. Words to be learned and understood include *perpendicular, congruent, quadrilateral,* and so forth. Terms such as *square root* and *improper fraction* must be understood, as well as various abbreviations and mathematical symbols.

Comprehension skills require that the student be able to select significant details, follow directions, recognize sequence and main ideas, and read various charts. Further up the scale in the higher level skills the student must be able to analyze information, synthesize ideas, and evaluate.

In science a highly technical vocabulary is introduced. The student encounters many new words such as *photosynthesis, oxidation, catalyst,* and so forth. He must also learn the scientific meanings of common words such as *velocity, energy, force,* and *work,* as well as new terms such as *astronaut.*

Comprehension skills require in addition to recognizing main ideas and significant details such factors as recording information in outline form, collecting data, classifying, and assuming cause-effect relationships. At the higher skills level the student must be able to synthesize ideas and to evaluate.

Specialized vocabulary in the social sciences includes such terms as *democracy, capitalism, imperialism,* and so forth. Then there are those common words with special meanings in the social sciences, for example, *left, right, cabinet,* and *bill.* The student learns also how new words are coined or how they enter the language (for example, *smog, SALT,* and *NATO*).

The comprehension skills include all those mentioned in this chapter with special emphasis on selecting important details, noting sequence, classifying convergently, making outlines, and reading maps, charts, graphs, and other pictorial aids. At the higher reading levels pupils are required to analyze information and propaganda, to recognize fallacies in reasoning and logic, and to be able to synthesize ideas and to evaluate.

Reading Rate

At the secondary level speed of reading or reading rate takes on added importance to the young adult. With so many reading assignments, a student with a slow, plodding approach will have difficulties. Fluency in reading and efficiency in rate can and should be developed. Some schools have special programs for average or better than average readers who want to become superior readers. Such a program is usually called developmental reading or advanced reading. If your teenager's skills in reading are average or better than average for his age level, then you should encourage him to select developmental reading as an elective course if such a program is offered at his school.

Reading rate includes reading comprehension. Actually the rate of reading is the rate of comprehension. Reading hundreds of words per minute is a waste of time if full comprehension is not achieved. Unless one is skimming or scanning for a particular purpose in reading, inclusive reading requires at least ninety percent comprehension.

Many claims have been made about certain speed-reading programs. Such programs have an appeal to young adults and may be very beneficial. As a parent you should have some basic information regarding speed-reading so that you may guide your teenager intelligently. His best option for improving his reading is to enroll in a course at the high school. In the event that he wishes to enroll in a course offered outside the public school, you should know some basic information about reading rate.

If you are reading this in the normal fashion, instead of progressing smoothly across the column, your eyes are moving in a series of fits and starts. Reading takes place as the eyes move along a line of print in a series of stops called *fixations*. The split-second movement when the eyes travel from one stopping point to another is called the *interfixation*. Because it's a jerky action it's also called a *saccade* or a *saccadic* movement. Then with the return sweep, also a saccadic movement, the eyes swing back across the page to start reading a new line of print.

One movement you probably can't detect is an involuntary action when the eyes backtrack a little and stop with a reverse fixation. These regressions shouldn't be confused with the conscious reviewing involved in rereading a phrase or sentence. All readers make these regressions by force of habit, perhaps the result of inaccurate perception.

Speed-reading is generally based on the theory that the amount of print read at one stop can be stretched to take in an eyeful of words or the whole of a written line. Using the "look" method, the reader moves his eyes straight down the page without shifting from left to right across each line. The theory claims that by focusing on the center of the line of print, a reader's peripheral vision will take in the words on both sides of the fixation point.

Unfortunately, the facts about perception don't cooperate with the claims of certain speed-reading advocates. A person could have 180 degrees of peripheral vision but that won't allow him to see a line of type at a glance. When the reader focuses on some point in a line of print, he sees at most only four or five letters on either side of the fixation point even with the sharpest perception. The letters farther away from his focus point are not at all clear. A person with normal vision focusing on a three-and-one-half-inch line of type (ten words), sees fifty percent less detail and clarity only a half inch away from the fixation point. An inch away the degree of perception drops to thirty percent. All of this simply means that even the best readers can only see and read an average of two or two-and-one-half words per fixation. The span of recognition shrinks when the reading involves unfamiliar concepts or vocabulary and increases with easy reading. But that maximum of a couple of words is hardly enough to support the contention that you can read in phrases or whole lines of print with each eye stop.

Another factor to be considered is the time it takes to read. Vision is clearest when the eye stop is around one-fourth of a second, although the fixation can be cut to about one-sixth of a second. The interfixation jump takes at least one-thirtieth of a second but research has shown that reading only takes place when the eyes aren't moving. In one study projected images were electronically activated so that they appeared only when the readers' eyes moved and disappeared when the eyes came to a stop. None of the subjects involved saw the material shown while their eyes were moving.

Taking those rates into account, is it possible to read 2,000 words a minute? Let's assume that a reader has the shortest possible fixation, the shortest interfixation, a maximum eye span of three words, and has no regressions. Even under these optimum conditions, the reader clocks in at only 15 words per second— 900 words per minute. Any rate above that is simply skimming or scanning and thereby eliminates large portions of material.

To study the act of reading, modern instruments (ophthalmographs) photograph the pattern of eye movement and produce an accurate graph of the path the eyes take. The subject sits in front of the device with his head held steady by a brace. As he reads the material in front of him, a small bead of light is directed to a point on the cornea of each eye. The beads of light are reflected off the corneas, through lenses and onto a continuously moving strip of thirty-five millimeter film. The tracing of the film caused by the reflected light results in a reading graph or eye movement photograph.

Using these instruments, readers who surpass eight hundred words per minute have been studied and have been found to be reading selectively. They peruse only parts of lines and actually skip complete lines. But when reading means covering most or all of the words on a page, then it's impossible to read inclusively more than nine hundred words per minute.

Graduates of speed-reading programs have also been tested. While they claim to be reading at several thousand words per minute without missing words or losing comprehension, the reading graphs don't agree. In one study of graduates of a popular program, the pattern on the photographs didn't show a high level of reading ability in a regular, systematic pattern or even a straight vertical line. Instead the graphs revealed a typically arhythmical pattern similar to those produced during skimming or scanning tests. No one in the study was able to read 5,000 or 6,000 words per minute with any reasonable comprehension. Those demonstrating the highest rates had the lowest comprehension—an average of 45 percent of the material read. When the examiner insisted on higher comprehension, the subjects reverted to conventional patterns of reading with their eyes rhythmically moving from left to right across the page and read under 1,000 words per minute.

The evidence against speed-reading doesn't depreciate the value of trying to improve one's reading skills. Vocabulary building, for example, continues to develop over a lifetime. But it is highly unlikely for one to develop a phenomenal increase in reading rate.

We have seen how vocabulary development, comprehension, and rate of reading fit into the total academic program of the adolescent. This multiplicity of skills is developed during the secondary school years through a variety of methods and techniques. Much of this instruction is achieved through the various subject areas that your teenager is studying. Where students are experiencing difficulty with one or more of the specific reading skills, help is provided through the school's reading improvement effort.

Programs in reading at the secondary school are usually offered at three levels depending upon student needs. The three types of programs are developmental, corrective, and remedial. A brief description of each type of program will serve to illustrate the reading instruction provided by the schools.

Developmental Reading

This type of program has as its main objective the enabling of students to develop their maximum reading potential.

The program is designed for students who are reading at grade level or better, and who need to continue developing their reading skills to meet the demands of secondary education, as well as preparation for higher education.

The training is provided to reinforce those reading skills developed during the elementary school years; it provides for an extension and continuum of essential reading experiences. This includes further instruction in the basic skills of vocabulary development, word analysis, rate, and comprehension. The program also provides for advanced training in applying reading to the various content fields. The program develops higher level skills in reading for study, critical reading, and advanced organizational and reference skills. In many instances this program is organized through the English and/or social science departments.

Corrective Reading

Corrective reading techniques are usually employed in a special reading class. Students in corrective reading are generally deficient in just a few of the essential reading skills. These deficiencies are diagnosed by the school's reading specialist and specific instructional techniques are prescribed for the student. Corrective reading instruction may last only a few weeks or it may last for the entire school year. The length of instruction depends on the nature of the reading deficiency. Once the deficiencies are corrected, the student should be able to adequately handle his academic coursework.

Remedial Reading

Remedial work is necessary when the student has experienced serious difficulty in reading. Students in need of remediation are usually diagnosed as being two or more years retarded in reading. This means that the student is seriously behind in most of the essential skills of reading. Remediation focuses on intensive instruction and drill in the development of reading skills.

If your teenager has a history of poor reading development he will probably need the help that can be provided through the remedial reading program. The school counselor and the reading specialist should be consulted to determine whether or not your youngster would benefit from such instruction.

Chapter 8

Teenage Reading Problems and What to Do about Them

Perhaps it's no wonder that so many teenagers experience some difficulty in the development of reading skills at the secondary level. In our modern society there is a great deal of competition for the student's time. Even youngsters without learning problems are often faced with difficulties in their studies because of the extent and variety of extracurricular activities such as sports, clubs, societies, and social events. It is not unusual for students with a record of top grades to suddenly find those grades slipping because of too many activities. If this is the only factor interfering with academic progress it can often be resolved by developing priorities for these activities. If a student bites off more than he can chew, something has got to go. And it's usually one or more extracurricular activities that must be forfeited.

Some teenagers experience difficulties with one or more of the essential reading skills. When a youngster is often frustrated in his attempts to read, he begins to hate the activity altogether. He then prefers to do almost anything except read. His school achievement suffers and he must then face the consequences of academic failure.

A part of the seriousness of reading disability in adolescence is the length and frequency of failure which the teenager experiences. To have reached adolescence without having developed sufficient reading skills usually implies that the student has experienced failure in the past and has probably been exposed to some type of remediation. Chances are good that such a teenager has been in remedial classes for a number of years. This fact should not discourage the student or his parents. A close look at the record over the years will undoubtedly indicate that measurable progress has been taking place and the youngster should be encouraged by this progress. Probably the most rewarding experience for a student is the success he achieves in his academic endeavors. The student's teacher is equally rewarded as he too experiences success in the teaching process.

One thing is fairly certain in remedial education—most children can and do respond to the instruction, and do make measurable progress. So it is therefore worth the effort involved in working toward overcoming deficiencies in reading. The student must be able to recognize his strengths and to build upon them. Where there are deficiencies, these need to be pointed out by an understanding teacher who is skilled in the ways needed to help the student to improve.

The problems that most adolescents with reading deficiencies face are generally tied in with a lack of suitable reading material. Youngsters are apt to encounter materials that are so difficult for them that they develop a defeatist attitude. In fact they go out of their way to avoid reading. In addition to his involvement in school activities and possibly a part-time job, the adolescent is also faced with the problems of growing up and becoming an adult. He needs more than ever to be accepted by his peers, and he is developing strong relations with people outside the family, such as teachers and friends. He is at a point where he is becoming more independent and must begin to break the kind of family ties which were part of his childhood. This spreading of wings spells the beginnings of independence. It is no wonder that the adolescent becomes confused. As a child his parents told him what to do. Now that he is becoming independent he must make some of his own decisions that will affect his life.

This maturing experience coupled with difficulties in reading can cause the adolescent a great deal of stress. At some point it becomes difficult for parents to understand why their child doesn't read. No matter what suggestions they make the adolescent rejects them. What the parents see as having little importance might be extremely important to the youngster. Forcing him to read will probably cause hostility and be of no value in the long run. The best thing that parents can do in this type of situation is to try to create an environment conducive to reading.

Factors in the Home

There are several approaches that may be employed in getting a teenager to read. Providing him with a relatively quiet background is almost essential. This means that brothers and sisters should not distract him during certain periods. Television sets and stereos may have to be turned down or off. In addition to relative quiet, some sort of schedule might be set up. Any schedule should of course be flexible; any duties and responsibilities assigned the teenager should have their place in a reasonable schedule. But the child should not be called upon in the middle of his reading to perform a household task, to wash the car, or to mow the lawn.

Having plenty of interesting materials around the house is of paramount importance in encouraging a teenager to read. As we have noted repeatedly in this book, working with a child's interests is the best method of stimulating a desire to read. Your own sensitivity to your child's needs should guide you in selecting materials to have around the house. If your choices are accurate and appealing to your child, he may eventually seek out further material on his own.

A basic characteristic of adolescence is a desire to learn more about oneself. This is often accomplished through learning about other people—their lifestyles, their thinking and philosophies, their approach to the problems of life, and so forth. Reading materials such as stories of family life that will help an adolescent to understand himself and his problems are usually well received. The school library has a variety of pamphlets dealing with real life problems and how people adjust to them. There are also numerous pamphlets dealing with self-improvement and how-to categories of vital interest to teenagers. The school librarian may be very helpful to a child in terms of the selection of suitable materials.

In addition to the areas mentioned adolescents enjoy books they may find on their parents' shelves. Some of the titles can serve as an introduction to adult reading. Teenagers enjoy such authors as Thornton Wilder, Pearl Buck, F. Scott Fitzgerald, and H. G. Wells.

Games played at home can serve to enrich a youngster's vocabulary and comprehension skills. Teenagers are stimulated by such games as Scrabble, cryptograms, crosswords, and double crostics.

Problems in Reading

Problems in reading during adolescence generally stem from difficulties experienced during early childhood and the elementary school years. In the diagnosis of reading disabilities the examiner tries to determine the causes of the problem. If the cause of the problem is understood the prescription for remedial instruction can be more easily developed. Unfortunately the cause of the problem cannot always be determined. It's possible, however, to find out what the deficiencies are so that they can be dealt with effectively.

The Reluctant Reader

The reluctant reader is the child who can read but won't. Naturally this constitutes a problem since a lackadaisical attitude interferes with the necessary continued growth in reading development. There are several possible reasons for the resistance to reading exhibited by the typical reluctant reader. He may be rebelling against school or parental standards or demands for reading. If these are too stringent he may develop an "I don't care" attitude. In this way he seeks to get back at parents and other adults for what he believes are unfair demands. On the other hand he may be highly energetic or even hyperkinetic and as such may find it difficult to settle down to reading. Still another cause of the reluctant reader might be that he lacks some of the fundamental skills of reading and therefore experiences difficulties which tend to frustrate his efforts.

Whatever the problem, one should keep in mind that there are reasons why the child is a reluctant reader. When we discover those reasons we can help the child to read independently and willingly. Some of the best methods in working with the reluctant reader include the provision of much easy and interesting material around the house. This material should include books, magazines, and reference sources. Interesting discussions at the dinner table about current events and recommended books also help.

Poor Comprehension

A slow rate of reading comprehension is a common problem among teenage remedial readers. There are many possible causes for this problem. Poor reading instruction in the early grades might very well contribute to reading deficiencies during the teenage years. Other factors include general lethargy, immaturity, and inner conflict. Even such factors as environmental conditions during infancy and the preschool years can contribute to the problem.

As additional contributing factors to reading problems one has to consider home and school conditions. Unfavorable home conditions include sibling rivalry, poor parent-child relationships, and family pressures to succeed at school. These conditions may contribute to a poor self-concept and general feelings of inferiority. Poor conditions at school can contribute to a teenager's reading difficulties. Overcrowded classrooms, double sessions, and other such conditions tend to compound reading problems. When the child enters high school his desire to improve in reading is intensified. It is at this point that he realizes the importance of reading in adult life and sometimes he feels that it is too late to do anything about the problem.

In working with teenage reading problems both parents and teachers must maintain a sensitivity to adolescent needs, particularly to the individual. This includes the child's learning ability, maturity, self-concept, and his relationships with others. As we mentioned in the preceding chapter, both the junior and senior high schools have specially developed programs for the improvement of reading. You should consult with the appropriate school officials—the counselor, reading teacher, assistant principal—relative to your child's needs. You may be able to determine the extent of your child's problem and the school's ability to help him to overcome or minimize his difficulties. If the problem is extensive, a nearby university reading clinic or a private tutor may be in the best interests of your child. The school will be able to help you by making suitable recommendations. As a parent, your interest and encouragement are needed. Your child needs to know that you recognize his efforts and his successes.

Questions and Answers

My teenager's school offers special courses in reading. How do I know what course would be appropriate for him to take? A school may offer programs in developmental, corrective, and remedial reading. Usually the school administers group achievement tests on a periodic basis. These test results indicate what reading program, if any, your child should be in. In general, students who score two or more years below grade level are advised to take remedial reading. Naturally if it is suggested that your child take a remedial reading class you should encourage him to do so. Where there are programs of corrective and developmental reading, the school will probably inform you of these opportunities for your child. You should not hesitate to contact your child's guidance counselor to determine which reading program your child should take.

How can reading help my teenager to solve his problems? By reading novels, short stories, and biographies about adolescent problems, the young adult learns about himself. He finds out through books that his peers may have similar problems and that he is not alone in the struggle of growing up. Boys and girls of this age are interested in books that deal with real life situations—good grooming, choosing a career, dating, courtship, marriage and family life. Through this kind of reading teenagers are helped in achieving their developmental tasks.

Is there a relationship between reading disability and juvenile delinquency? It is difficult to pinpoint a specific relationship between difficulty in reading and juvenile delinquency. However, there have been many cases of delinquency brought before the juvenile court in which a history of reading disability is indicated. These are the youngsters who cope with their failure in aggressive ways. Their poor achievement in school may lead to truancy, which in turn allows them time to get into trouble. Case studies have demonstrated instances where improvement in reading resulted in improved behavior.

Books for Parents

Alm, Richard S., ed. *Books for You*. New York: Washington Square Press, Inc., 1964.

Anderson, Verna D. *Reading and Young Children*. New York: Macmillan, 1968.

Arbuthnot, May H. *Children's Reading in the Home*. Glenview, Ill.: Scott, Foresman, 1969.

Beck, Joan. *How to Raise a Brighter Child*. New York: Trident Press, 1967.

Bond, Guy L. *Teaching the Child to Read*. New York: Macmillan, 1966.

Carlsen, G. Robert. *Books and the Teenage Reader: A Guide for Teachers, Librarians, Parents*, 2nd ed. New York: Harper, 1972.

Dodson, Fitzhugh. *How to Parent*. Los Angeles: Nash Publishing, 1970.

Duker, Sam. *The Truth about Your Child's Reading*. New York: Crown Publishers, 1956.

Durkin, Dolores. *Children Who Read Early*. New York: Teachers College Press, Columbia University, 1966.

Emery, Raymond. *High Interest-Easy Reading for Junior and Senior High Reluctant Readers*. Champaign: National Council of Teachers of English, 1965.

Fader, Daniel N., and McNeil, Elton B. *Hooked on Books: Program Proof*. Berkeley: Medallion Books, 1968.

Fenner, Phyllis. *The Proof of the Pudding: What Children Read*. New York: John Day, 1957.

Ginott, Haim G. *Between Parent and Child*. New York: Avon, 1965.

Greenberg, Kenneth, R. *A Tiger by the Tail: Parenting*

in a Troubled Society. Chicago: Nelson-Hall Publishers, 1974.

Ilg, Frances L. *School Readiness.* Evanston: Harper, 1965.

Johnson, Edna. *Anthology of Children's Literature.* New York: Houghton, 1960.

Larrick, Nancy. *A Parent's Guide to Reading.* New York: Doubleday, 1969.

Monroe, Marion. *Growing into Reading.* Glenview, Ill.: Scott, Foresman, 1951.

New York Public Library. *Books for the Teen Age.* New York: The New York Public Library, annually.

Nicholsen, Margaret. *People in Books.* New York: H. W. Wilson, 1969.

Pilgrim, Geneva H. *Books, Young People, and Reading Guidance,* 2nd ed. New York: Harper, 1968.

Roos, Jean Carolyn. *Patterns in Reading,* 2nd ed. Chicago: American Library Assn., 1961.

Solomon, Doris, Comp. *Best Books for Children.* New York: R. R. Bowker, 1970.

Spache, George. *Good Reading for Poor Readers,* rev. ed. Champaign: Garrard, 1974.

Strang, Ruth. *Gateways to Readable Books.* New York: H. W. Wilson, 1966.

Thomison, Dennis, Ed. *Readings about Adolescent Literature.* Metuchen, N.J.: The Scarecrow Press, Inc., 1970.

Todd, Vivian E. *The Years before School, Guiding Preschool Children.* London: Macmillan, 1970.

Tooze, Ruth. *Your Children Want to Read.* Englewood Cliffs, N.J.: Prentice, 1957.

Walker, Elinor, Comp. *Book Bait.* Chicago: American Library Assn., 1969.

Walker, Elinor. *Doors to More Mature Reading.* Chicago: American Library Assn., 1964.

Books for Children

Picture Books

Adoff, Arnold. *Black Is Brown Is Tan.* New York: Harper, 1973. Ages 4-8.

Barton, Byron. *Jack and Fred.* New York: Macmillan, 1974. Ages 4-7.

Blegvad, Lenore, ed. *Mittens for Kittens.* New York: Atheneum, 1974. Ages 4-6.

Bodecker, N. M. *It's Raining Said John Twaining.* New York: Atheneum, 1973. Ages 3-8.

Brandenberg, Franz. *Fresh Cider and Pie.* New York: Macmillan, 1973. Ages 4-6.

Brown, Marcia. *All Butterflies, an ABC.* New York: Scribners, 1974. Ages 4-6.

Charlip, Remy. *Harlequin and the Gift of Many Colors.* New York: Parents' Magazine Press, 1973. Ages 5-8.

Clifton, Lucille. *All Us Come Cross the Water.* New York: Holt, 1973. Ages 5-9.

de Paola, Tomie. *Nana Upstairs and Nana Downstairs.* New York: Putnam, 1973. Ages 4-8.

Deveaux, Alexis. *Na-Ni.* New York: Harper, 1973. Ages 6-9.

Jeffers, Susan. *All the Pretty Houses.* New York: Macmillan, 1974. Ages 4-7.

Keats, Ezra Jack. *Pssst! Doggie.* New York: Watts, 1973. Ages 4-8.

Kotzwenkle, William. *The Supreme, Superb, Exalted and Delightful, One and Only Magic Building.* New York: Farrar, 1973. Ages 8-11.

Langstaff, John. *The Two Magicians.* New York: Atheneum, 1973. Ages 4-8.

Lear, Edward. *Whizz!* New York: MacMillan, 1973. Ages 4-8.

Lobel, Anita. *A Birthday for the Princess.* New York: Harper, 1973. Ages 5-8.

McDermott, Gerald. *The Magic Tree, a Tale from the Congo.* New York: Holt, 1973. Ages 5-8.

Marshall, James. *Yummers!* New York: Houghton, 1973. Ages 4-6.

Pomerantz, Charlotte. *The Piggy in the Puddle.* New York: Macmillan, 1974. Ages 3-5.

Preston, Edna M. *Squawk to the Moon, Little Goose.* New York: Viking, 1974. Ages 3-5.

Provensen, Alice. *Our Animal Friends at Maple Hill Farm.* New York: Random, 1974. Ages 4-6.

Pyle, Howard. *King Stork.* Boston: Little, 1973. Ages 4-8.

Raskin, Ellen. *Who, Said Sue, Said Whoo?* New York: Atheneum, 1973. Ages 4-6.

Rice, Eve. *Oh, Lewis!* New York: Macmillan, 1974. Ages 3-6.

Rockwell, Anne. *Befana: A Christmas Story.* New York: Atheneum, 1974. Ages 4-6.

Rockwell, Harlow. *My Doctor.* New York: Macmillan, 1973. Ages 3-5.

Rounds, Glen. *The Day the Circus Came to Lone Tree.* New York: Holiday House, 1973. Ages 6-9.

Shulevitz, Uri. *Dawn.* New York: Farrar, 1974. Ages 4-6.

Shulevitz, Uri. *The Magician.* New York: Macmillan, 1973. Ages 5-8.

Tobias, Tobi. *A Day Off.* New York: Putnam, 1973. Ages 5-8.

Tripp, Wallace. *A Great Big Ugly Man Came up and Tied His Horse to Me.* Boston: Little, 1973. Ages 4-8.

Veno, Noriko. *Elephant Buttons.* New York: Harper, 1973. Ages 3-up.

Wells, Rosemary. *Benjamin and Tulip.* New York: Dial, 1973. Ages 4-6.

Zemach, Harve. *Duffy and the Devil: A Cornish Tale.* New York: Farrar, 1973. Ages 5-8.

Zolotow, Charlotte. *Jamey.* New York: Harper, 1973. Ages 4-8.

Fiction

Anderson, Lonzo. *Izzard.* New York: Scribners, 1973. Ages 5-9.

Babbitt, Natalie. *The Devil's Storybook.* New York: Farrar, 1974. Ages 9-12.

Bell, Frederick. *Jenny's Corner.* New York: Random, 1974. Ages 9-12.

Blume, Judy. *Blubber.* Scarsdale, N.Y.: Bradbury, 1974. Ages 9-12.

Byars, Betsy. *After the Goat Man.* New York: Viking, 1974. Ages 9-12.

Child, Lydia M. *Over the River and through the Wood.* New York: Coward, 1974. Ages 6-9.

Cohen, Barbara. *Thank You, Jackie Robinson.* New York: Lothrop, 1974. Ages 9-12.

Di Fiori, Lawrence. *A Toad for Tuesday.* New York: Lothrop, 1974. Ages 6-9.

Fox, Paula. *The Slave Dancer.* Scarsdale, N.Y.: Bradbury, 1973. Ages 11-12.

Fritz, Jean. *Why Don't You Get a Horse, Sam Adams?* New York: Coward, 1974. Ages 6-9.

Goffstein, M. B. *Me and My Captain.* New York: Farrar, 1974. Ages 6-9.

Greenfield, Eloise. *Sister.* New York: Crowell, 1974. Ages 9-12.

Himler, Ronald. *Little Owl: Keeper of the Trees.* New York: Harper, 1974. Ages 5-9.

Hoban, Lillian. *Arthur's Honey Bear.* New York: Harper, 1974. Ages 6-9.

Holman, Felice. *Slake's Limbo.* New York: Scribners, 1974. Ages 9-12.

Jones, Hettie. *Coyote Tales.* New York: Holt, 1974. Ages 8-12.

Lorenzo, Carol L. *Mama's Ghosts.* New York: Harper, 1974. Ages 9-12.

Munson, Tunie. *A Fistful of Sun.* New York: Lothrop, 1974. Ages 8-12.

Peck, Richard. *Dreamland Lake.* New York: Holt, 1973. Ages 10-14.

Smith, Doris B. *A Taste of Blackberries.* New York: Crowell, 1973. Ages 7-10.

Smith, Doris B. *Tough Chauncey.* New York: Morrow, 1974. Ages 9-12.

Stolz, Mary. *Land's End.* New York: Harper, 1973. Ages 10-12.

Thomas, Marlo. *Free to Be ... You and Me.* New York: McGraw-Hill, 1974. Ages 9-12.

Ungerer, Tomi. *Allumette.* New York: Parents' Magazine Press, 1974. Ages 6-9.

Young, Jim. *When the Whale Came to My Town.* New York: Knopf, 1974. Ages 6-9.

Nonfiction

Adkins, Jan. *Toolchest: A Primer of Woodcraft.* New York: Walker, 1973. Ages 9-up.

Aliki. *The Long-Lost Coelacanth and Other Living Fossils.* New York: Crowell, 1973. Ages 4-8.

Burchard, Marshall. *Sports Star Tom Seaver.* New York. Harcourt, 1974. Ages 6-10.

Cole, Joanna. *Dinosaur Story.* New York: Morrow, 1974. Ages 6-10.

Collins, Patricia. *Motion.* New York: McGraw-Hill, 1974. Ages 8-up.

De Pree, Mildred. *A Child's World of Stamps.* New York: Parents' Magazine Press, 1973. Ages 8-up.

Fenner, Carol. *Gorilla, Gorilla.* New York: Random, 1973. Ages 8-12.

Hayes, Wilma P. *Foods the Indians Gave Us.* New York: Ives Washburn, 1973. Ages 9-12.

Horwitz, Elinor. *Mountain People, Mountain Crafts.* New York: Lippincott, 1974. Ages 9-12.

Jackson, Robert. *Joe Namath, Superstar.* New York: Walck, Inc., 1974. Ages 8-12.

Kalina, Sigmund. *Your Blood and Its Cargo.* New York: Lothrop, 1974. Ages 7-11.

Kaufman, Mervyn. *Jesse Owens.* New York: Crowell, 1973. Ages 6-9.

Klein, Stanley. *The Final Mystery.* New York: Doubleday, 1974. Ages 3-5.

Kurelek, William. *Lumberjack.* New York: Houghton, 1974. Ages 9-12.

Macaulay, David. *Cathedral.* New York: Houghton, 1973. Ages 10-up.

MacClintock, Dorcas. *A Natural History of Giraffes.* New York: Scribners, 1973. Ages 10-12.

Monjo, F. N. *Poor Richard in France.* New York: Holt, 1973. Ages 6-9.

Pace, Mildred M. *Wrapped for Eternity: The Story of the Egyptian Mummy.* New York: McGraw-Hill, 1974. Ages 9-12.

Pratson, Frederick. *The Special World of the Artisan.* New York: Houghton, 1974. Ages 9-12.

Price, Christine. *Talking Drums of Africa.* New York: Scribners, 1973. Ages 8-12.

Rudeen, Kenneth. *Roberto Clemente.* New York: Crowell, 1974. Ages 7-9.

Sarnoff, Jane. *A Great Bicycle Book*. New York: Scribners, 1973. Ages 10-14.

Sheffield, Margaret. *Where Do Babies Come From?* New York: Knopf, 1973. Ages 5-8.

Silverstein, Alvin. *Hamsters: All About Them*. New York: Lothrop, 1974. Ages 8-12.

Silverstein, Shel. *Where the Sidewalk Ends*. New York: Harper, 1974. Ages 9-12.

Books for Teenagers

Aiken, Joan. *Midnight is a Place*. New York: Viking, 1974. Ages 12-16.

Bach, Alice. *Mollie Make-Believe*. New York: Harper, 1974. Teenage.

Bacon, Martha. *In the Company of Clowns*. Boston: Little, 1973. Ages 11-14.

Brady, Maxine. *The Monopoly Book*. New York: McKay, 1974. Ages 12-up.

Brown, Dee. *Wounded Knee: An Indian History of the American West*. New York: Holt, 1974. Ages 12-up.

Bennett, Jay. *The Dangling Witness: A Mystery*. New York: Delacorte, 1974. Teenage.

Cleaver, Vera. *Me Too*. New York: Lippincott, 1973. Ages 12-14.

Collier, James L. *My Brother Sam is Dead*. New York: Four Winds, 1974. Ages 12-up.

Coolidge, Olivia. *The Apprenticeship of Abraham Lincoln*. New York: Scribners, 1974. Ages 12-up.

Cormier, Robert. *The Chocolate War*. New York: Pantheon, 1974. Ages 12-up.

Danziger, Paula. *The Cat Ate My Gymsuit*. New York: Delacorte, 1974. Ages 10-14.

Duncan, Lois. *Down a Dark Hall*. Boston: Little, 1974. Ages 12-up.

Fenton, Edward. *Duffy's Rocks*. New York: Dutton, 1974. Teenage.

Fine, Reuben. *The Teenage Chess Books*. New York: McKay, 1974. Ages 12-up.

Garfield, Leon, ed. *Strange Fish and Other Stories*. New York: Lothrop, 1974. Ages 12-up.

Goldstein, Kenneth K. *New Frontiers of Medicine*. Boston: Little, 1974. Ages 12-up.

Hamilton, Virginia. *M. C. Higgins, the Great*. New York: Macmillan, 1974. Ages 11-15.

Hyde, Margaret. *Mind Drugs*. New York: McGraw-Hill, 1974. Teenage.

Jackson, Jacqueline. *Turn Not Pale Beloved Snail*. Boston: Little, 1974. Ages 12-up.

Konigsburg, E. L. *A Proud Taste for Scarlet and Miniver*. New York: Atheneum, 1973. Ages 11-15.

Levy, Elizabeth. *Lawyers for the People*. New York: Knopf, 1974. Ages 12-up.

Lightner, A. M. *The Space Gypsies*. New York: McGraw-Hill, 1974. Teenage.

Lyle, Katie L. *Fair Day, and Another Step Begun*. New York: Lippincott, 1974. Teenage.

McHargue, Georgess, Comp. *Hot and Cold Running Cities: An Anthology of Science Fiction*. New York: Holt, 1974. Ages 12-up.

McNeill, Janet. *We Three Kings*. Boston: Little, 1974. Ages 12-up.

Mazer, Harry. *The Dollar Man*. New York: Delacorte, 1974. Ages 12-up.

Montgomery, L. M. *The Road to Yesterday*. New York: McGraw-Hill, 1974. Teenage.

Murray, Michele. *The Crystal Nights*. New York: Seabury Press, 1973. Ages 11-16.

Myers, Walter D. *The World of Work: A Guide to Choosing a Career.* New York: Bobbs-Merrill, 1974. Ages 12-up.

Nourse, Alan E. *The Bladerunner.* New York: McKay, 1974. Ages 12-up.

O'Dell, Scott. *Child of Fire.* New York: Houghton, 1974. Ages 11-15.

Pryce, Dick. *Safe Hunting!* New York: McKay, 1974. Ages 13-up.

Reeder, Col. Red. *Bold Leaders of WWI.* Boston: Little, 1974. Ages 12-up.

Rinaldo, C. L. *Dark Dreams.* New York: Harper, 1974. Teenage.

Robertson, Keith. *In Search of a Sandhill Crane.* New York: Viking, 1973. Ages 11-15.

Roth, Arthur. *The Iceberg Hermit.* New York: Four Winds, 1974. Ages 12-up.

Sachs, Marilyn. *The Truth About Mary Rose.* New York: Doubleday, 1973. Ages 10-14.

Scott, John A. *Hard Trials on My Way.* New York: Knopf, 1974. Ages 12-up.

Wells, Rosemary. *None of the Above.* New York: Dial Press, 1974. Teenage.

Whelan, Elizabeth. *Sex and Sensibility.* New York: McGraw-Hill, 1974. Teenage.

Index

Adams, Richard, quoted, 6
Adroitness, physical, 41
Affiliated Publishers
   (N.Y.), 26
Aggressiveness, childhood, 11
Alphabet
   games to learn the, 64–65
   teaching the, 28
*American Folk Songs for
   Children* (Seeger), 26
Astigmatism, 19, 21
Attention span, child's, 40

Basal reader, 53, 71
Basal reader approach, 54–57
Bingo reading game, 63
Binocular coordination, 19
Books for enjoyment, 54

Boys Choir, 26
Brain damage, 7–8
Brain function, faulty
   patterning of, 8
Bureau of Research of the
   U.S. Office of
   Education, 6

Comic books, 79
Compound words
   game, 74–75
Comprehension
   poor, 103–4
   skills of, 86–89
Context, meaning
   through, 84
Convergence, eye, 21
Corrective reading, 97

117

*Counting Games and
    Rhythms,* 26
Cross-eyedness, 21

Developmental
    reading, 96–97
Developmental
    tasks, 18–22, 38–39
*Developmental Tasks and
    Education*
    (Havighurst), 18
Diplopia, 21
Double vision, 21
"Dyslexia: A Discussion of
    Its Definition," 6
Dyslexia, definition of, 5–10

Educational Testing Service
    (Princeton, N.J.), 47
Enthusiasm for reading, 12
Eye movements, faulty, 7

Federal Government's Attack
    on Dyslexia, 6
Fernald method of
    teaching, 9
Fixations, 93–94
Frustration tolerance, 10
Functional behavioral
    patterns, 10–11

Games
    as a help in phonics, 60–64
    prereading, 43–45
    for reading, 74–76
Gillingham method of

teaching, 9–10
*Give Your Child a Head
    Start* (Lewis), 26
Golden Records, 26

Havighurst, Robert,
    quoted, 18
Hearing difficulties, 25
High schools,
    reading in, 83–98
Hyperactive child
    syndrome, 10
Hyperkinetic syndrome, 10
Hyperopia, 19, 21

Individualized Reading
    Instruction, 69
Initial Teaching Alphabet, 59
Intermediate grades, reading
    in the, 70–79
International Phonetic
    Alphabet, 59
Interpretation of reading
    matter, 16
Irritability, childhood, 11
It's a Small World, 26

Juvenile delinquency and
    reading ability, 105

Karloff, Boris, 26

Language experience
    approach, 57–58
Language factors, 41–42
Learning the ABCs and

How to Count (Rice), 26
"Learning to Read," 47
Levinson, Sam, 4
Lewis, Shari, 26
Linguistics approach, 58–59
Listen, ability to, 25–26
Look-say method versus
    phonics, 46–47
Low frustration tolerance, 10

McGuffey readers, 54
Mann, Horace, quoted, xi
Massachusetts Board of
    Education, xi
Mathematics, reading
    in, 92–93
Mental abilities, 41
Mexican children, reading
    ability of, 51
Minimal brain dysfunction, 10
Motivation, a child's, 40
*My First Golden Record
    Library*, 26
Myopia, 19

National Education
    Association, x
National Reading Center
    (Washington, D.C.),
    8, 64
Nixon, Marni, 26

Overactivity, 10

Parents
    educational responsibility

of, ix–x
    help afforded at home
        by, 11–12
    reading ability influenced
        by, 4–5
Partnership reading
    game, 65–67
Perceiving, 16
Personality, a child's, 41
Phonetic-alphabet
    approach, 59–60
Phonetic approach to
    reading, xi
Phonics, 38
    games to help in, 60–64
    phonetics distinguished
        from, 48–50
    the teaching of, 50–53
    versus the look-say
        method, 46–47
Phonics approach, 58
Phonograph records as an aid
    in listening, 25–26
Physical adroitness, 41
Physical skills, 23–24
Pitman, Sir James, 59
Poems for the Very Young
    (Nixon), 26
Poor readers, number of, x
Prereading experiences, 28–29
Prereading games, 43–45
Primary grades, reading in
    the, 37–69
Problem readers, x
Programmed learning
    approach, 60

Readiness
  how to achieve reading,
    42–43
  to read, 38–42
Reading
  comprehension, 93, 103–4
  definition of, 15–17
  learning of, 30–33
  as a problem, 3–14
  teenage deficiencies, 99–105
Reading and spelling, 78–79
Reading development of the
    child, 12–13
Reading interests, range
    of, 72–73
Reading rate, 93–96
Reading test scores, 76–77
Recognition, child's need
    for, 4
Remedial reading, 97–98
Rhythms of Childhood, 26
Rice, Rosemary, 26
Robinson, Francis, 89

School as a gratifying
    experience, 27–28
Schools
  instructional responsibility
    of, ix
  visiting the, 42
Science, reading in, 92–93
Secondary school reading,
    83–89
Seeger, Pete, 25
Seeing and reading, 16
Sentence completion game, 44

Sight, problems of, 18–21
Skills, primary reading, 53–54
Snellen Chart, 21
Social sciences, reading in
    the, 92–93
Spanish versus English
    sounds, 51
Speed-reading
    programs, 93–96
Spelling and reading, 78–79
SQ3R study formula, 89–92
Studying, skills used in, 89–92
Structured analysis, 50

Talking
  learning of, 24
  reading as an extension
    of, 30–32
Teenage reading problems,
    99–105
Ten pins game, 65
Textbooks, 53–54
Three Little Pigs
    (Karloff), 26
Toys, value of, 23, 24, 27
Treasure hunt, 63

Underachiever, 11
Understanding of what one
    reads, 16

Vision, the child's, 18–19
Vocabulary development,
    teenage, 83–85

Walking, learning of, 23–24

Walleyedness, 21
Walt Disney Songs, 26
Word building game, 98
Word games, 60–67, 74–76
Word recognition skills, 47–50

Word rummy, 75
Word wheel, 61
Words in Color alphabet
    system, 59